What people are saying about
The Anatomy of Accomplishment

Bravo! So many gems in this book. These 19 interesting and unique female entrepreneurs offer us sage advice that I wish I had at the beginning of my own journey. That said, each of their stories has inspired me to become a better version of myself today.
— Matthew Ferry, Author, *Quiet Mind Epic Life*

The words and advice on the pages of this book represent the culmination of grit, failure, success, joy, finding passion and being authentic while building sustainable businesses. About women, by women, the messages are ones that make us take pause, see ourselves in these writers and understand that our feelings of strength and vulnerability are felt by women across generations, geographic locations and business types. Best of all, the women you will meet in this book are honest. In a world where everyone wants to come across as perfect, these women give us their best, share their shortcomings and dare to be human. They acknowledge the need for balance, the inclusion of family and the value of lessons learned. As a CMO of a mid-market organization, I already have put my highlighter to good use—the benefits of this material are scalable for companies of all sizes and for women at every point in their careers.
— Donna Erbs, Chief Marketing Officer,
Anders CPAs + Advisors

So, you want to be an entrepreneur? That's a fantastic career choice but one that should come with a clear-eyed warning. It's a tough road. One that's filled with reward and risk, autonomy and long hours, and of course success and failure. It's my experience that the most effective personal development for the entrepreneur is spending time learning from peers. This is a must-read book for any entrepreneur that details the challenges of building the company and lifestyle you want—from those that have been there and done that. The real-world stories here provide honest perspectives on what to expect as you begin the journey. They provide deep insight into various business, family and personal hurdles faced and how the entrepreneur overcame them. Most importantly, you will discover what they learned along the way.

– Dino Signore, PhD, President, The Signore Group

These authors have successfully built their "why" and are ready to help champion yours. Page after page has been crafted to deliver specific, actionable steps the reader can use to drive their "why" forward and produce results. This book delivers opportunities for success that my clients and my sales team alike can learn from. Now is the perfect time to make The Anatomy of Accomplishment *part of your daily reading to craft your success!*

– Dan Iadevito, Vice President, Business Banking,
Enterprise Bank & Trust

This book is an inspiration; I was actually moved to tears with some of the stories! With grace, authenticity and courage, 19 diverse women entrepreneurs share their trials and triumphs that have led to expert business advice. Erin Joy says, "It's not important what you call it, vision, commitment or purpose, what's vital is that it calls to You." In each of their stories, it's clear the author is called to her work for a higher purpose.

– Amy S. Narishkin, PhD, Founder, Empowering Partners

The book brings together many different success stories which have one thing in common: strong and amazing women determined to succeed. Each and every author describes the incredible journey she went through to become a successful business owner. These stories, full of devotion and dreams, helped me to reignite my own passion. Thank you, authors, for your professionalism, thought generosity, and courage to share your experience!

– Margarit Khachatryan, Founder & CEO, MagAnalytics

Yes, "Bigger, Better, Bolder" is behind every word in this book and has set a fire in my belly that has been dormant! I'll no longer sit and wait, fearful of the unknown. Instead, I will take a leap into that fear, knowing that even if I fail, my truest, highest results are but a mere a step away! I'm ready to release all my magic and gifts to the world! Thank you for the passion and care offered in these stories— I am inspired!

– Kesha Kent, BA, MAOL, CEO and Founder,
MrsKeshSpeaks, Author, Networking it's a SuperPower

This powerhouse book reflects the energy that Erin breathes into her consulting practice as she mobilizes entrepreneurs to break through the inevitable headwinds. Each author offers a credible mental framework for the reader to progress with actionable steps. Using the experiences of these authors, entrepreneurs will be well-served to take these lessons learned within their own wheelhouse to learn, grow, and adapt on their own path to success.

– Edward Lott, Management and Leadership Professor,
Team Lead, Commercial Real Estate Services,
Cushman & Wakefield

THE ANATOMY OF ACCOMPLISHMENT

Your Guide to Bigger, Better, Bolder Business Results

The Anatomy of Accomplishment
Your Guide to Bigger, Better, Bolder Business Results
Compilation by Erin Joy, PhD Candidate, CEO of Black Dress Circle

Published by Black Dress Circle, St. Louis, MO

Publishing Consulting, Project Management, and Interior Book Design: Davis Creative, daviscreative.com

Strategy and Cover Design Concept: Arco + Associates, arcoandassociates.com

Library of Congress Cataloging-in-Publication Data

Library of Congress Control Number: 2020900660

Erin Joy

The Anatomy of Accomplishment:
Your Guide to Bigger, Better, Bolder Business Results

ISBN: 978-1-7345111-0-9

Library of Congress subject headings:

1. BUS109000 BUSINESS & ECONOMICS / Women in Business
2. BUS025000 BUSINESS & ECONOMICS / Entrepreneurship
3. BUS046000 BUSINESS & ECONOMICS / Motivational

ATTENTION CORPORATIONS, UNIVERSITIES, COLLEGES AND PROFESSIONAL ORGANIZATIONS: Quantity discounts are available on bulk purchases of this book for educational, gift purposes, or as premiums for increasing magazine subscriptions or renewals. Special books or book excerpts can also be created to fit specific needs. For information, please contact Erin Joy, Black Dress Circle, erin.joy@blackdresscircle.com.

Table of Contents

Dedicated to women entrepreneurs and executives that hustle daily all over the world.

Acknowledgments

First, I am thrilled to acknowledge the 18 other authors who joined me in writing this book. Without their willingness to share hard-won wisdom and experience so generously this project would still be just an interesting idea. Each author included here is a model of the creativity American business thrives on, and each also exemplifies what is possible when women business owners cooperate, collaborate and celebrate each other's successes.

Then, of course, there is Andrea Arco, the marketing mastermind who never misses a chance to enhance her clients' presence in the marketplace. Andrea brought the concept of this book to me from Cathy Davis, of Davis Creative. Whenever Andrea recommends that I do something, I usually do it, and never regret it. That was the case with *The Anatomy of Accomplishment*. I barely had time to say, "Okay, let's do it!," and Andrea was designing the book cover! She and I have collaborated on every aspect of publishing this book, from concept development, to the strategy for securing writers, from author support, through production, to the book launch itself.

Without Shannon Redling, my business partner extraordinaire, this book could not have been realized. Shannon supports the foundation of our business and keeps the wheels turning smoothly, empowering me to pursue our dreams. She holds the vision for Black Dress Circle as passionately as I do, and has worked continuously alongside me to bring it into reality. Shannon focuses on doing the right things, in the right way, strengthening the platform we stand on. And, through all the plates she spins, she always sees the target clearly—the best possible service to our clients.

Also, I'd be painfully remiss if I didn't acknowledge my confidant and personal wordsmith, Cathy Soete, with whom I share a decade of experience, self-expansion, and camaraderie. Cathy has an astonishing ability to reach into the depths of my mind, harvest my ideas, develop them with me, and distill my thoughts into just the right words that most powerfully communicate my message. She continually makes me a better leader and a better person, and empowers me so I can empower others.

Finally, my thanks and acknowledgment to Cathy Davis of Davis Creative. She created the anthology series business model, of which this book is a part, as a means of promoting and supporting women business owners around the world. Your expertise allowed us to bring *The Anatomy of Accomplishment* from concept to bookshelf. Your leadership allows women everywhere an opportunity to participate in the empowering world of entrepreneurship.

How Strategic Thinking Steers My Business to Success

*Success is the progressive realization
of a worthy goal.*

–Earl Nightingale

I wasn't born strategic. At twenty-two years old, just out of college with a marketing degree, I entered the industry that promised the most independence—real estate. My early career was filled with plenty of phone dialing and zero strategic thinking.

Twenty-four years later, everything I do in my coaching and consulting business is strategic—planning, scheduling, hiring, networking...you name it.

How did I make the transition from random action to meticulous game plan? In 2012, St. Louis-based marketer Andrea Arco and I met for coffee to explore how we could mutually benefit from each other's expertise. Before we had finished our lattes, we were creating a *twenty-five-year plan* for the business of my dreams.

Seriously.

I understand that you might not be interested in creating a business plan as far-reaching as mine. But by the time you finish reading this chapter, I promise, you will know eight strategic levers for moving your business as far as you want it to go.

The Turning Point

There is always a moment in a person's career where events take a critical turn, even when we're not aware of it at the time. For me, it happened after I left real estate sales for housing construction. The building industry was booming, creating new, profitable opportunities. I was young and ambitious, and my goal was to become a leading consultant for home builders—specializing in sales, marketing, and organizational development.

To lay a foundation of knowledge and personal connections, I researched building industry publications, highlighted the names of people who advertised themselves as marketers, and started cold calling them. On one call, I hit it off immediately with the owner of a Washington, DC-based company. He understood the business niche I wanted to fill and generously offered to teach me everything he knew about the housing industry and the support services it needed.

We worked together, long distance, for three years; and with his mentoring, I positioned myself in St. Louis as a coach for housing developers, offering sales and organizational workshops to hundreds of beginners and mid-career people in the industry. I kept myself really busy with that and might have continued on that path for a long time except for two things: The housing collapse of 2008 and the fact that the lifestyle of the industry—long hours and little sleep—was taking a toll on my well-being. My crisis point rose where those two realities met.

To stay in business and restore my health, I needed to adapt my coaching services to a broader array of industries. And with the social media revolution raging, I also needed to start reaching beyond in-person, place-based audiences.

The decision to expand my client base ignited my imagination. Having kindled a passion in the building industry for leading workshops and events, I now pictured myself on national and international speaking tours, websites, podcasts, electronic and print publications, Facebook groups, and TV and radio interviews.

With these images dancing in my head, I went to that pivotal lunch where Andrea Arco advised me that such an expansive vision would require an extensive plan. Our process was to look toward the end result I desired and work backwards to where I currently was.

Through the past nine years of building Black Dress Circle—seven of those with Andrea by my side—I've learned that hope doesn't keep a long-term plan alive. I now think strategically about every aspect of my company. These eight aspects became my levers of success.

Eight Success Levers for the Strategic Entrepreneur

I list these aspects according to how crucial each is to overall success. At different times they may vary in importance, but they always interweave with each other.

Vision. What does your business bring to the marketplace? Ice cream or cleaning products? Accounting services or pet grooming? As an entrepreneur, you're free to offer the market anything you choose. But there's also always something *intangible* behind what you sell. That intangible is the vision, or driving idea, that had you go into business in the first place.

Sometimes new entrepreneurs are concerned that their vision isn't large enough, or creative enough. But in my view, if you can answer the simple question, "Why do you want to have your own business?" then you have the core of your vision. Maybe you want to make a comfortable income for your family. Or provide jobs in the community. Or have fun while making a product people enjoy or admire. You might call it your "commitment" or "mission" or "purpose." What you call it isn't important. But it is vital that it calls *to you.*

I knew early on that I loved coaching people, speaking to groups, conversing with people about their businesses, being known as someone who has something valuable to say, and bringing interesting people together. From my doctoral studies in business psychology and my own experience in the market, I also knew that there was a scarcity of support for women entrepreneurs.

Over time, as I talked with two of my coaches about how to bring my projects into sharper focus, I realized that one main passion was driving me: My vision is that my work advances the success and empowerment of women entrepreneurs worldwide. From my one-on-one coaching, to my Black Dress Circle round-tables, to speeches, workshops, podcasts, and writing for publication, this idea energizes everything I do. That is what a clear vision can do for you. It gets you out of bed in the morning, pulls you into action, and motivates you to take risks. It can also give you the satisfaction and fulfillment that you seek.

As my career continues to grow and expand, I'll invent more ways to accomplish my vision. But my strategic thinking and decision making will be done with the same driving force in mind. If you create and focus upon your vision, you'll eliminate needless doubt, enjoy a purpose for *all* of your work, and have your hands on a key lever for executing your strategic plan.

Team. Gathering the right people to work with you is critical. And challenging. Your business may require a team of one hundred, a team of two, or some number in between, but each single person must play a role in fulfilling the vision—even if they're only with you for a short time. If you don't surround yourself with the right team members who are willing and able to execute your plans, compliment your style, and shore up your weaknesses, you can't build a successful business.

I've had success with my team members because I give time and thought to selecting the right person for a job, even if it takes longer than I'd like. My company runs lean, and that means every staff member has to be versatile, flexible, and able to think critically.

One team member, who was with me for three and a half years, was someone I observed for several months while she was working on a volunteer board before I approached her with a job offer. She demonstrated the technology skills, temperament, and flexibility I needed in a team member. Plus, she understood how I like to work and what I want to accomplish with every project.

My overseas team member, who has been with me since my real estate days, is brilliant with technology, marketing, communication, processes, and scheduling. She's like an extension of my brain—able to conceptualize and build upon my vision while offering alternatives and opposing perspectives when warranted. When she moved thousands of miles away, our partnership was so solid that we decided to make every accommodation to maintain it, even across seven time zones.

When my clients are choosing team members, I remind them of the old rule of thumb: "Hire slow and fire fast." Occasionally, I've had clients who are reluctant to dismiss employees even when they are damaging the productivity, morale, or integrity of the company. I coach them, not too gently, that it makes no sense to jeopardize success simply to avoid dismissing someone who isn't a good match for your company. Once you commit to building and maintaining the *right* team, it strengthens your resolve and allows you to make hiring and termination decisions with greater clarity and less stress.

Advisors and Coaches. Not everyone believes that having a key group of advisors and coaches is crucial to performance. Some entrepreneurs just hope that savvy professionals and wise peers will show up at the right moment. I beg you not to count on that. A small- to medium-sized company can't afford to keep every resource in-house, or put every necessary professional on the payroll. This is why I place trusted advisors and coaches high on my list of strategic levers. When you choose your accountant, marketer, attorney, technology firm, banker, and other outside professionals, you're making them a part of your team. If you don't vet and cultivate them as carefully as you would an employee, you have a gaping hole in your strategy.

On the risk side, if you bring in advisors without great care, you could be entrusting your financial assets, intellectual property, and other resources to people who don't have your best interests at heart. On the opportunity side, you could be missing out on the collateral benefits that come with trusted relationships, such as ad hoc advice, and access to new resources and networks.

Besides professional experts, it's crucial to gather a core group to whom you can turn for advice or coaching. If I need an objective perspective or access to immediate high-caliber talent, I turn to one or more of "my people." When I produced the Midwest Women Business Owners' Conference (MWBOC) for three years, I gathered a group of women who had years of experience in event planning, production, and public speaking. As our work on the conferences accelerated, these core members reached out to other experienced individuals to create our team. Without their assistance, the conferences could not have succeeded.

I also often turn to videographers, caterers, designers, and others whom I count on for specialized expertise. As you build networks in your community (see Lever # 5) you'll find that small business owners will often accept compensation through the exchange of in-kind services.

Timeline. Think of the strategy of a timeline by imagining billiard balls on a pool table. Any pool player can take a shot at the ball closest to a pocket. The strategy comes in when a player sees an opportunity to set up two or three shots ahead of time. This, of course, takes patience and flexibility. The situation on the table changes quickly and unpredictably, just like situations in your business. As the architect of my long-term plan for Black Dress Circle, I am free to make appropriate changes whenever needed. And I do.

Often, I'm invited to engagements that would give me positive exposure, perhaps in a city where I hope to expand my franchise. If I approach my work as though aiming to put one ball in a pocket at a time, I might just take such opportunities as they come. But that's a linear way of managing a timeline, and it could lead to my schedule being dictated by random influences, rather than strategy. On the other hand, always holding rigidly to your plan isn't good either. An opportunity might be so advantageous that it's worth rearranging a budget, a schedule, or your entire business plan. For example, if your advertising budget is set, but you're presented with a good project that requires money, it's smart to see what can be adjusted in your ad timeline. Immediately tossing out the original plan isn't wise, but you might find an alternative route that allows you to respond to the opportunity.

Andrea Arco and I routinely look for national speaking opportunities. Although keynote speeches are an integral part of my long-range business plan, we may decide that, in this or that instance, it wouldn't be wise to pursue a speaking engagement when I have several other projects in motion.

Thinking strategically gives you a longer view. An advisor can help you determine how one action will match up with whatever else is going on. Seeing how all of your initiatives interact allows for coordinated—not disjointed—movement.

Networks. There's no question that women business owners get emotional support from socializing with peers and associates. I often used to gather with colleagues just for the pleasure of talking business after hours. That, however, is not strategic networking. When you have a strategy for networking, you gain much more than a social connection. Networking should provide you with reliable access to the resources you need in a timely way.

The owner of a small company—with a tight staff, tighter budget, and broad responsibilities—operates at a major disadvantage if she does not cultivate expansive networks that share business information and contacts. We entrepreneurs can be so driven by our desire to be independent that we sometimes isolate ourselves from the resource-rich groups that are in our own backyards and beyond. One of my coaches likes the police acronym BOLO, "Be On The Lookout." That's a cue to keep an eye out for people in my networks who could fulfill a specific need for myself or a client.

A key theme of my second Midwest Women Business Owners' Conference was "What Do You Need? Who Do You Need?" It's vital to put these questions out there wherever entrepreneurs and executives gather. My clients, associates, and friends know that I have a strategic purpose whenever I bring people together—I unabashedly ask people to come ready to engage in substantive conversations about what they do, what their vision is, and what and who they need as resources. The more we share and collaborate, the better the outcome for everyone. The way we stay successful and relevant in our markets is to always bring as much *or more* value to our networks as they give to us.

Of course, supportive friendships may form at networking events, but it's vital to remember that their strategic purpose is to create communities of business women *who can and do* share ideas, talents, products and services with each other.

Technology. Having to learn how to use IT tools can be a turnoff for those of us who want to focus on our field of expertise rather than become a techie. The bad news is, unless your product or service is highly siloed and geographically concentrated, the wise use of technology *must* be a key part of your business strategy. The good news is, if you're smart enough to start your own business and care enough about it to be reading this book, you're capable of learning how to reap the benefits of the technology you need. Technology is not my thing, but my comfort level with cloud-based tools for communication, data storage, scheduling, and budgeting is growing.

When I hired two of my team members, I was most impressed by their technology skills. I needed their expertise and wanted to learn from them. You can do the same with your team. If you have just one tech-savvy team member, you have your launching point. Technology pros have an aptitude for learning and applying new programs and processes as you need them. Just as importantly, with an IT professional on board you have an in-house translator who can work with the wide world of tech geniuses out there.

In early 2015, my team and I decided to purchase a software package that had more capacity than we needed. It was one of the smartest things we could have done. Today, as our contact lists constantly grow, we have an in-house data storing, sorting, and communicating ability to serve us for years to come.

If I wasn't thinking strategically from the perspective of our long-range plan, I wouldn't have considered such an investment. My vision of building a global network through which to empower women entrepreneurs is only possible with outreach tools. International speaking tours, online courses, virtual roundtables, and more, all require targeted communications before, during, and after.

Your business, like mine, depends on attracting, maintaining, and expanding our client and customer relationships. Technology is the vehicle that will allow us to keep extending our reach. (And we've barely begun to envision how artificial intelligence will impact our lives and businesses!)

Marketing. This strategic lever is so critical that it seems too far down the list. But the fact is, marketing only works when other essentials are in place. The product or service first has to be developed in such a way that it can fulfill what the marketing plan promotes.

Entrepreneurs are an ambitious and self-confident lot. Left on our own, we might be convinced that fast growth and new, shiny marketing ideas are the best path forward. Unfortunately, many marketers get derailed by this reactive marketing—they get distracted by a new technology or a new promise or a new partner without remembering an essential element: All marketing strategies should work to support business goals. If a marketing strategy cannot be directly tied to one of your main business goals, it's probably not worth the time or investment. By keeping your business goals top-of-mind, you're more likely to create a proactive marketing strategy that moves you forward.

If *you and your expertise* are what you plan to sell, the preparatory steps run parallel to selling an object. Like me, you have to be willing to view yourself and your skills as the product.

My collaborative work with Arco+Associates offers a demonstration of how strategic marketing is a step-by-step process: We are aiming for a national and international stage. Yet, to start, we focused on local audiences: St. Louis radio programs, feature interviews and event promotions on TV shows, print publications, Facebook groups, and podcasts.

Every event, speech, and award is thoughtfully publicized through media that reach my target audiences. This publicity is intended to build recognition and legitimacy in my current and future marketplaces.

This book you're reading is intended not only to provide expertise and information to you, the reader, but also to build visibility for future speaking engagements. My presentations have a two-fold purpose: One is to contribute value to the audience; and the other is to continue to expand the demand for what I have to offer as a coach, consultant, thought leader, franchisor and speaker. Make your efforts have dual purposes—make them multi-task as effectively as you do.

The PhD I will earn in the coming year, not only proves my scholarship in the field of business psychology, but also provides a platform for greater credibility and impact in a noisy marketplace. Depending on your goals, your business may not require as extensive a marketing strategy as mine. But if you have a product or service to sell, strategic marketing must be an integral aspect of your plan.

Well-being. I hate placing well-being last on my list of strategic levers, fearing readers might assume it is least important. But without well-being as a high priority, a business owner absolutely cannot fulfill a long-term plan. If I didn't have personal experience with chronic illness, I'm not sure if I'd be so adamant about protecting well-being. It's one thing to hear and read about the problems caused by lack of sleep, poor nutrition, and harmful habits, but it's quite another thing to learn when you're young that your lifestyle is debilitating.

Late nights, unhealthy food and drink, and little exercise did not seem unusual to me. They seemed to be the habits of almost every other young business woman I knew. But those habits, for me, are gone for good. The diagnosis of a chronic auto-immune disease four years ago has dictated a sleep, diet, exercise, and stress management regimen that I view as a vital lever of success.

My plea to you, regardless of your experience with health issues, is that you consider your well-being to be the most powerful and empowering aspect of your life. When you take the time to get seven or eight hours of sleep, eat foods that fuel you, exercise regularly, and replenish your mind and spirit, you're maintaining the one instrument that allows you to do *everything* else.

I know. Women business owners—who are often also wives and mothers—say they don't know where to find the time to take care of themselves. But while you can delegate many projects and tasks to your employees, you are the *only* one who can care for your well-being.

In order to manage the strategic levers that will lead you to success, you need to have these traits: physical and mental energy, a clear head, stable mind-set, calm demeanor, patience, decisiveness, a sense of humor, and the ability to handle situations with flexibility and resilience. If you're lacking sleep and nutrition, are in pain, anxious, tense, uncomfortable, or chronically worried, you won't have the traits you need, when you need them. I don't tell my clients when to sleep, what to eat and drink, or what to do for relaxation. Every person has to figure that out for herself, or with a health coach. *Just find a way.*

Yes, but. What I've offered here is practical coaching from someone who keenly observes the realities and needs of women business owners. But *you are the one on the field.* You get to make the plays.

You might say, "I find the idea of a plan to be confining. I want to go more with the flow."

Remember, you get to create the plan. If you feel too boxed in by it, create one that gives you more freedom.

You might say, "I don't like a plan that is too long range."

Make it shorter. Try it out for six months, a year, five years.

You might say, "I don't want to grow nationally or internationally. I like working in smaller areas."

So keep your business local. Concentrate on the industry or region in which you feel confident.

You might say, "I find the idea of having a strategy for everything is too much to wrap my head around."

Don't overcomplicate it. Call it your plan or your guideline, or name it something that propels you to create instead of recoil in a state of overwhelm.

Yes, it does take patience and discipline to approach a business with strategic thinking, but it *will* gradually take root if your vision inspires you.

For me, the more clearly I can see where I am headed, the more satisfying each step on the journey becomes.

 A strategic consultant, trusted confidant, and straightforward advisor, Erin Joy has made it her life's mission to provide female business owners with the resources, services, and support they need to be successful in business and life. She is founder and CEO of Black Dress Circle®, a facilitated, member-driven entrepreneur roundtable program where women business owners discuss issues, share experiences, frame decisions, and leverage collective knowledge alongside others who understand the unique challenges of managing emerging and evolving companies. This program has improved the productivity, efficiency, and profitability of organizations across many industries, and is currently being franchised to other women in other markets.

Erin has received multi-year recognition as a top consultant in the St. Louis area, was twice designated one of the top 100 St. Louisans to know and received the Enterprising Women of the Year Champion Award in 2019. She received a Master of Arts in human resources management from Washington University in St. Louis and is currently pursuing her Ph.D. in business psychology from The Chicago School of Professional Psychology.

erin.joy@blackdresscircle.com
www.blackdresscircle.com

www.facebook.com/erinjoy.blackdresscircle
www.instagram.com/erinjoy.blackdresscircle
www.linkedin.com/in/erinjoy

At the Core of Creation is Courage

My professor once said, "Courage is the most important of all the virtues, because without courage you can't practice any other virtue consistently. You can practice any virtue erratically, but nothing consistently without courage."

That professor just happened to be award-winning poet, author, and activist, Maya Angelou.

At twenty-six years old, I had no concept of the valor that would soon be required of me as I began my journey as an entrepreneur. In the corporate world, I had worked with agencies and I had experience in the agency world working with clients. From all sides, it was clear that the agency model needed to be revamped and if I wanted it to be done differently, I would be the one doing it.

It was 2005 and the economy was great. I had no idea that a recession was just around the corner, during which marketing would be the first thing most businesses would cut. I didn't know how rare profitability was for a small agency like mine (in 2018, out of thousands of agencies surveyed in twenty-four countries, thirty-two percent reported less than ten percent of net profit margin in the prior twelve months, and many reported a loss). I was not expecting that this new city that my husband and I had found ourselves in—St. Louis, Missouri—would be one of the toughest markets to break into.

In retrospect, I'm grateful I did not have any of that knowledge. I was relying solely on my confidence in the business I wanted to create and the impact it could have. This confidence bred courage, and courage is at the core of creating a sustainable, successful business.

As I approach my fifteenth year in business, I am getting the "how did you do it?" question—an inquiry that makes me uncomfortable. Yes, I've created a successful, sustainable business in an ultra-competitive industry; but there are many layers to this journey and countless pieces that make up the ever-evolving puzzle that is business success. At the core, though, is courage.

Do I have it all figured out? Hell no. But I've learned a few things that could help business owners and executives as they discover and harness their unique courage to make their own impact on the economy and the world.

Six Sentiments for Sustainable Success

1. Stay true to what makes you unique.

When I moved to the Midwest from the East Coast, I quickly realized that anyone who met me knew I wasn't from here. As an outsider, I had two options: I could learn all of the inside lingo, conjure up a more mellow midwestern style, and try to blend in; or, I could embrace my fast-paced persona, share my unique perspective, and let my true identity attract those who would appreciate it. I chose the latter and have built so many beautiful relationships because I did.

The choice to stay true to what makes me unique translates directly to the success of my business. When I started my business, I did so with the mentality that I could and would do things differently than any other agency. I focused every initiative around the client's goals rather than my own gain. I provided added value and on-the-house consultation every chance I could get. I leveraged my business savvy as a way to cut through the creative noise.

Today, those passion-driven differentiators haven't wavered, and my clients reap the benefits. Because I was able to identify that unique value and remain true to it for nearly fifteen years, the community in which I was once an outsider has now embraced me and Arco + Associates.

*Actionable Tip:*Think back to when you had the initial idea for your business or career and identify where the passion came from. Then, keep that driver top of mind during every business decision you make and every message you put into the world.

2. Don't lose perspective.

As a young entrepreneur, my life at times was consumed by my business. When something didn't go according to plan, I let it affect me personally. When work was good, life was good—but shouldn't we be striving for happiness throughout every inevitable ebb and flow of business? (Yes, we should.)

When I became a mother, I was forced to step back and see the big picture. While I've always been comprised of many "layers"— wife, daughter, friend, creative, athlete—it was the mom layer that helped me see the value in acknowledging every piece of my identity. I also had to slow down and embrace the perspectives—and paces—of these tiny humans. With the view that I am more than my professional self, that success is a self-made definition, I can better approach both the highs and lows of business and life.

If you can find balance within each layer that makes up the whole you—and a level of integration amongst your "selves"—you can leverage positivity to remain courageous and competitive in your business.

Actionable Tip: Make a pie chart of all the pieces thatare part of you. Think in percents about how frequently you identify with each piece of yourself and adjust the percentages accordingly. How can you make this more equal? How can you shift your perspective to give each of those pieces the respect they deserve when things go wrong?

3. Allow for flexibility, without comprising integrity.

My company's mission is to make an impact on businesses of deserving clients across the nation by solving marketing challenges and creating and executing innovative, results-oriented marketing strategies. In order to do this, we must continually evolve, remain flexible, and be ready to pivot when goals shift.

Additionally, my company is inflexible when it comes to our core values. One of our values is to focus every initiative around the client's goals rather than our own. I put my client's needs first and am confident that, at the end of the day, integrity is key to long-term sustainability.

There have been countless scenarios, for example, in which a client has asked us to implement an initiative that I did not believe would produce results or would compromise our beliefs. Because I always want to produce results for clients, I have no problem turning down revenue in order to remain in line with my values.

Actionable Tip: Create a culture deck—a slideshow or document that breaks down your company's culture, core values, and mission into clear, easy-to-absorb pieces—and refer back to it frequently to ensure all business decisions are aligned. Then, once a month, set aside time with your team to make a list of ways you've acted accordingly. What has made you proud? If you can't think of anything, use that time to plan for improvement in the future.

4. Get serious about hiring high performers.

If I could do one thing differently over the past fifteen years in business, it would be to hire sooner. I waited ten years to hire my first full-time employee. But when I did decide to take the leap and put my faith in the talent of others, I went all in. Every hire I have made in the past five years has been extremely intentional with a focus on cultural fit.

High-performing employees aren't easy to come by. So much of the workforce is looking for a gig where they can clock in, get their work done early with plenty of internet-browsing time to spare, and clock out. Those aren't the type of workers who are going to thrive in the company culture I've created.

To combat this, we've adopted the "slow to hire, quick to fire" adage. We do our best to ensure cultural fit before hiring by utilizing personality assessments, having candid discussions throughout the interview process, and working with human resources consultants and recruiters. To attract top performers, we've gotten creative with nontraditional benefits. Most importantly, I have no problem parting ways with an employee who doesn't end up fitting the mold.

Actionable Tip: If you don't have a stringent process in place for hiring, get started on it now. Outline granular steps, from search to onboarding to employee reviews and evaluations. A good starting place is to think about the process you used for the employees that didn't work out and work backwards to see how you can improve next time.

5. Never get comfortable.

Marketing is a competitive industry. Rather than resting on my laurels when things are going well, I use that time to get strategic and prepare for the company's next evolution.

Case in point: I didn't follow a strategic marketing plan for my company until about a year ago. That may seem counterintuitive as a marketing firm, but we were focused on our clients, not on us. I realized, though, that the kind of long-term sustainable growth I'm aiming for requires more than word-of-mouth referrals. Now, we work with sales consultants; we have business development processes; and we've created and implemented a marketing strategy much like we do for our clients.

Actionable Tip: Remember that what got you here won't get you there. If business is going well right now and operations are running smoothly, get focused on planning for the future. What new alliances can you begin to build? How can your team be even more productive? How can you turn your employees and top customers into brand ambassadors?

6. Practice the Shine Theory.

Shine Theory is a term coined by journalist and podcaster Ann Friedman that promotes the practice of mutual investment with the simple premise that "I don't shine if you don't shine." It describes a commitment to collaborating with, rather than competing against, other people—especially other women.

I heard Friedman share about the Shine Theory at a conference a few years back, and it really spoke to me. In my younger years, I had many great mentors and inspiring colleagues, but also saw my fair share of women purposefully stifling other women in the workplace. I've seen firsthand that competition does not lend itself to a culture of collaboration. Now that my team is growing consistently, I try to keep this in mind. Any opportunity to promote teamwork, provide positive feedback, or share the glory is an opportunity to create the rising tide that lifts all boats.

Actionable Tip: Take stock of how each of your team members is motivated. While some prefer public recognition and praise, others may respond better to additional responsibility and under-the-radar acknowledgments. Learning and leveraging what makes each individual work harder is a surefire way to make your entire team shine.

Final Thoughts

Writing this chapter has been an interesting exercise. While listening to companies' histories and growth trajectories and diving into the reasons for success or failure are all part of the marketing deep dive we perform for prospective clients as we begin to create a marketing strategy, it has been interesting to turn the mirror around and really see myself and my company.

As a senior at Wake Forest University (my undergraduate alma mater), Dr. Angelou invited her dramatic poetry students to her house in Winston-Salem, NC. It was the end of the semester and we had all dressed up for the occasion. Her signature booming laugh rang out throughout the halls of her home as she visited with students. As she glided from room to room what struck me was how real she was; her authenticity no doubt one of the many attributes that had contributed to her success. She had the courage to be herself—all of herself—and that was powerful. As she floated to where I was sitting with friends, she put my final poem in front of me. At the top, in maroon, it read, "I see you through this piece. Well done."

Thus, I end where I began, echoing a legend I was lucky enough to know.

I see you, entrepreneurs and business owners and executives. I see you through what you are creating, and I say well done.

 Andrea Arco-Mastromichalis is the founder and CEO of Arco + Associates, LLC, a marketing communications firm based in St. Louis, MO that serves clients nationwide. Prior to starting Arco, Andrea directed the marketing efforts at two Boston-based law firms, held senior copywriter positions at advertising agencies along the East Coast, and worked as the Marketing Director at The University of Virginia's Engineering School.

She has been published in *The Boston Business Journal, Women's Business, The National Law Journal, The Pittsburgh Business Times, and USA Today*. She graduated summa cum laude from Wake Forest University in Winston-Salem, NC with degrees in communications and journalism. She was the only Master's candidate to be awarded a full scholarship to the Corporate Communications program at Duquesne University. She is passionate about helping CEOs and business owners market their products, services, and brands with smarts and strategy.

She is a member of the *St. Louis Business Journal's* 40 under 40 class of 2016, a silver Stevie Award winner for female-led workplaces, an Enterprising Women Award Winner, and has been recognized by the *Small Business Monthly* as a Top Woman Business Owner.

aarco@arcoandassociates.com
www.arcoandassociates.com

Continued on next page

www.facebook.com/arcoandassociates
www.twitter.com/arcoassociates
www.linkedin.com/company/2424644/admin/
www.vimeo.com/user61794053

Playing for
the Long Game

I love the fact that I was one of the few women working in technology when I started my career. Early on, I witnessed women being promoted into executive positions and knew that my father's counsel to go into technology was a good choice. Technology doesn't care about race or gender. If you're good, you can advance. I was fortunate that I worked in large corporations and was exposed to some amazing training, best practices, and diverse work styles. The best practices were not lost on me and something that I continue to keep in mind with my own company: striving to be the best and constantly improving.

My training as a software developer started with a six-month internship with the Missouri Division of Family Services during my senior year in college. That experience helped me land my first job as a programmer for Russell Stover Candies. I moved from there to other large corporations headquartered in Kansas City. My career progressed, and I received promotions into senior and management positions. It was after the implementation of a major initiative that the first seed was planted to start my business.

My team had just implemented a corporate repository system to hold the data elements of four major divisions in a Fortune 500 company. I was approached by one of the employees in my group with the business model which would become my company, ECCO

Select. This co-worker thought that I had the ability to provide "that extra value" in an IT staffing company. The timing was important because we had deployed bleeding-edge technology that was one of the first intranets in a major corporation.

Our company had been known as a technology innovator which hired skilled resources, and my cohort had helped me understand the need for true technologists in the IT staffing industry. The importance of the business model hinged on the knowledge, skills, and experience that staff had toward understanding and implementing new technologies to help solve business problems.

It was a very different value than what the competitors in tech staffing were providing at that time. Most of the firms in our area hired salespeople with little or no technology knowledge. The competitors were not skilled in qualifying candidates to meet client needs, especially with emerging technologies. This left many clients yearning to trust someone who understood IT and find the right person, fast.

My business model came together after working on a business plan. I was fortunate to live in Kansas City, which is headquarters for Kauffman Foundation. This organization was created by an amazing entrepreneur, Ewing Kauffman. Mr. Kauffman was not only a successful pharmaceutical entrepreneur, baseball team owner, and philanthropist, but he created Kauffman Foundation to assist entrepreneurs in bringing their big ideas to life. I was given the advice that the Kauffman Foundation's FastTrac program could help me. And boy, did it ever.

After six weeks of spending Friday evenings and Saturday mornings with mentors and entrepreneurs, I evolved with a business plan. They helped me understand my assets, value my ability to find the right people, and be competitive with Big Four resources. All at a better value, a/k/a, lower price point. With a growing market need, technical specialists who understood the emerging technologies, and business consultants who could help determine how updating legacy systems could improve processes and modernize business applications, I moved forward with marketing my newly founded company, ECCO.

ECCO Select was incorporated as Elite Computer Consultants, "ECCO" for short. People have asked how I came up with this name. It was one of the few times that I've done any real marketing exercises. I had to think of how clients would find me. I knew that professionals in this industry would look up companies in the White Pages. I wanted the name of this new company to be early in the alphabet so that the name would catch the eye of potential clients. "Computer consultants" was a common term in that era, and it was a category in the White Pages. Not having much of an imagination, "Elite" was settled on to help distinguish the emphasis on the caliber of people we would serve. The "Select" part of ECCO was added in 1997 when I found that the Internet domain for "ecco" had already been taken.

Again, my marketing exercise was very simple. We marketed experienced resources that were the highest caliber in their discipline. Watching a commercial describing that the finest coffee beans were used in their "select" brand, I added the word; and ECCO Select not only became the new brand, but we bought the domain name as well.

I signed my first client in the winter of 1995 after a former employer reviewed my business plan and asked if I would consider coming back as a contractor to modernize an old batch system (keypunch cards). Subsequently, I became the first contractor for ECCO and wore all hats—billables, business development, recruiting, payroll, accounting, human resources, and marketing. We hired staff to accommodate this first client in modernizing old systems and addressing their bigger concern for the future; that is, Y2K, transitioning from 1999 to 2000.

Y2K was a valid reason to assess legacy systems and to scan every line of code that had a calculation involving dates. This had to be done to avoid shutdowns potentially created by the change from December 31, 1999, to January 1, 2000. This simple problem was a worldwide issue that everyone needed to address.

To understand the issue, we need to recognize that in tech's early days most people assumed all century dates began with the digit "nineteen." If programs assumed nineteen as the first two digits of the century, then everything from maintenance to payroll could be affected when the year 2000 began. Therefore, all date calculations needed the first two digits of the new century incorporated.

Back in the mid-90s, as computers began talking to each other via the world-wide Internet, businesses realized that they had more than one problem: not only Y2K, but also rethinking how their businesses could improve and potentially grow by using the Internet. Modernization efforts went into full-blown planning exercise. It was a period when a lot of time and money was spent to plan out what could be done to assess current systems, address problems, and determine solutions. We were entering into an era in which my services would be needed by almost anyone who had any type of custom or inhouse computer systems.

I am fortunate that I started at a time where there was a unique need and that I understood the technology and how to address the demand. As demand for technology specialists grew, so did our services. In the beginning, ECCO was doing very simple transactions: Get a client. Find out what they needed. Find candidates, present them. If a client was interested in any of the candidates, we'd follow with interviews and feedback. Hopefully, there would be an offer with a contract to place the candidate and they would be an ECCO billable consultant at the client site, with a specific deliverable and time frame. Typically, assignments lasted anywhere from three months to a year. If someone did what the client needed and the budget allowed, contracts were extended. This is what I did with my first client.

Those first few placements were easy as far as the back office. I did the selling, recruiting, placement, onboarding, invoicing, and quality control. But I only had one client. I learned the hard way that, just like financial investments, a company must have diversity. Having one client was like having all your eggs in one basket. My first client was my only client for almost two years. After the second year, that client claimed bankruptcy.

Fortunately, a couple of events kept the client's company afloat. They allowed my contractors to convert to full-time employees. Second, because I was a very small business and had a great relationship with senior executives, I was one of the first to be paid after the bankruptcy reorganization.

Lesson Learned:
Get Financing When You Don't Need It.

When my invoices weren't paid, I went to the bank to get a line of credit to pay my contractors, even though I didn't know when or if I might get paid. The bank would not give me the line of credit because my only account receivable was with a client in bankruptcy. So, my husband and I used our home as collateral to make payroll. After we were back on track, I made a point to know my banker and leverage his advice. Today, I have multiple banks wanting to loan me money. Occasionally, we use the line of credit, but it's typically due to timing.

Lesson Learned:
Stay in Touch with Former Associates.

With our first client in bankruptcy, and knowing that our bills would be paid, I sought a new opportunity. I was able to place a few of us with a previous employer — the Fortune 500 company where I had learned the most about intra/Internet protocols. I had kept in touch with the management team and employees. Staying in touch paid off!

Lesson Learned:
Leverage Past Performance.

After starting at our second client site, I knew I had to cultivate other potential clients. Working full time as a billable consultant made it a bit of a challenge. This client had four divisions where I could sell our services. And, I wanted to offer more than just supplemental staffing. I started responding to requests for solutions with statement of work responses. I found hired people who could address complex needs and provide very specific deliverables. These statement-of-work projects helped grow our brand and provide a past performance that allowed us to tell a more credible story to new prospects. That past performance also allowed us to enter into the public sector and diversify the type of clients we serve.

Lesson Learned:
Work on the Business, Not Just in the Business.

While working with our second client, I was presented with an opportunity to buy an IT permanent placement company. This acquisition not only helped me to scale but provided a diverse customer portfolio, systems, and infrastructure to support growth. It also added direct-hire placements to our offerings. I began to work *on* the business as opposed to working *in* the business.

We found that we could supply people who could handle large business transformations and people who had business skills beyond IT. For example, one of our clients needed resources to communicate changes. As an offshoot, we created a "Communications Office" and supplied resources to execute and direct changes. In addition to our other IT services, this enabled ECCO to begin offering organizational change management, program management, independent validation and verification, document storage solutions, training, and knowledge transfer in all types of organizations.

Lesson Learned:
Be Flexible.

I've always been open to offering new services. If these services do well, we expand and invest; if they don't, we must understand why it didn't work and what lessons were learned. Then we move on.

Growing a successful business year over year isn't enough. I want long-term success. I constantly challenge myself and my team. We ask, "Do our technologies, tools, policies, and people make sense for where we are today as well as where we want to be in three to five years?"

Since starting ECCO, we've weathered a client going bankrupt, embezzlement, theft, and the worst disaster of all: 911. What I've learned is that persistence, resilience, and resourcefulness all come into play when overcoming obstacles!

As the company has grown, so have I. Not just personally but professionally. The growth and success ECCO has experienced mirrors the success felt by our family, associates, clients, and the community. We have all benefited by doing our best and being proud of what we do. This is playing for the long game. Everyone benefits.

Jeanette Hernandez Prenger, Founder, President and CEO of ECCO Select, leads a Top 500 Hispanic business, with more than 300 employees serving clients throughout North America. ECCO Select is a talent acquisition and advisory consulting company, specializing in providing people, process, and technology solutions for clients, with offices in Kansas City, MO and Washington, D.C.

Jeanette progressed her career from software developer to management at major companies such as Sprint, TWA, Federal Reserve Bank, and Waddell & Reed. In 1995 she founded ECCO. It has grown into a leading provider of technology talent for Fortune 1000 companies and government agencies.

Jeanette is known for her community involvement, serving on the national boards of The Latino Coalition, Junior Achievement USA, Boy Scouts of America, Women Impacting Public Policy and Orphaned Starfish Foundation. Local board involvement includes the Federal Reserve Bank of Kansas City Economic Advisory Council, the Kansas City Convention and Visitors Association (Visit KC), the American Royal, Kansas City Tech Council and St Luke's North Hospital.

Jeanette is a graduate of Park University with a BS in Management Information Systems. She now serves as chair of their Board of Trustees.

jprenger@eccoselect.com
www.eccoselect.com

www.linkedin.com/in/jprenger
www.linkedin.com/company/ecco-select

Alyce Herndon

Path to Purpose

As an educator, mentor, and coach, I work with many women who create a path for themselves; and in watching them create, I, too, have been inspired to find my purpose. In the various roles that I occupy, my mission is to assist, guide, encourage, and motivate women to turn their passion into profits. Seems easy? Some days it is. It is most fulfilling when I work with women business owners who are in a creative space, offer guidance to support their goals, and celebrate accomplishments and victories when they appreciate the information shared, as they implement strategies that further impact their businesses.

Every day, I have the pleasure of meeting women who are in the idea, or pre-venture, stage. One thing I know is we all start with an idea. We attempt to define the concept and propel that idea into a profitable business. Another thing for sure is that every path is different. Basically, there is no set pattern that will be the same for everyone, except for the initial start-up process.

Most of my clients' conversations with me begin, "So, Alyce, I have this side hustle that I enjoy doing for family and friends, and I always give it away."

One client explained, "I create a meal for single mothers so they can eat with their children instead of going to fast-food restaurants. This serves as a way to bring families together reconnecting them to one another after a long day."

Great, you have just identified your target market, your vision, mission, and core value statement. I must share that every start-up concept is not always this simple. Sometimes it takes a little more conversation; but with guidance of a mentor or coach (such as myself), together, we can create a strategy which includes documentation of the idea. The goal is to take that idea or dream that is envisioned and make it a reality.

There was a lady who came to my office once. She had a notebook with the name of her business, her target market, and the clients she wanted to serve. She was still working a full-time job, which she was considering leaving to launch her new business. For years, she had served as an event coordinator. To remember every detail about the events she coordinated, she created an intake form; she knew what the clients wanted, had photos, and created a very detailed process. She even had a list of clients that were asking her to do weddings, birthdays, engagement parties, etc. However, with all she had documented, she was overwhelmed with fear. All of the "what-ifs" kicked in. What if they decide not to use my service? What if they don't want to pay? What if?

And I responded, What if they love your service? What if they refer others? What if?

As she looked at me, I reminded her, if you have the vision, there will also be provision. Let's grow!

An example of the idea-to-reality process is to identify what it is that you enjoy doing, or what it is that you do with little to no effort. In most cases, that very idea can move from being a spare-time concept to one that will create a job for yourself and others.

I call this a "strategy formulation." Strategy formulation is critical in the pre-venture stage and sets the foundation for the path on which the business owner will travel. As I assist small business owners with strategy formulation, it is important that they create a positive mind-set. How they think is very important. Just as the what-ifs set in with one person, it can become overwhelming, so it is imperative to have a notebook and to document your thoughts during the initial or pre-venture stage. As you document, various thoughts will continue to assist in formulating a strategy and in creating a timeline so you can begin the implementation process.

Strategy implementation is what I consider a process of beta testing. After we formulate a strategy, we have to test the steps to ensure we have a process that we can manage, to ensure that it works and is profitable. The goal is to lay the foundation, then identify the target market and research if what we are implementing will work. This will include the message that we want to communicate to potential customers, so we can also create a marketing campaign.

For example, I was working with a client, and I asked if she had a brochure, a website, or a communication she used with her potential clients? She said, "Well, I'm in business." I laughed, but she was serious. I said, "Okay, so let's talk it through." I had her tell me more about her business and then asked if she would write down her key services. As she notated her services, she grouped them and was able to create her message and craft her marketing campaign. We continued our discussion and I asked, "Where would you advertise? How will you create a stir about your services?" She shared that most of her clients were members from her church, and they also refer. Following my suggestions, she documented her list of clients and began asking them how they learned about her services. After hearing their responses, strategy implementation was born and the rest is growth.

Consistency is key. Once you start (strategy formulation), the goal is to continue to push through (strategy implementation), to create new ways, and assess what is working, then restart the process.

When working with women business owners who are in the pre-venture stage or initial stage, I like to listen to the story of their "Why?" I listen, because launching and running a business is a significant undertaking, and there are a variety of reasons as to why women decide to start a business.

As a doctoral student, my research is focused on women business owners who implement successful strategies. While exploring the background of challenges that women have encountered throughout their lives, I have found that women start businesses for a variety of reasons, including their personal desires of becoming business owners. Some women are forced to make hard decisions to ensure they have work-life balance; some women face involuntary factors. Motivation often begins as a way to achieve this balance in their work-life obligations, which may include family and having a support team that can give women the initiative to start a business and the strength to enhance their firm's performances.

Daily, I embrace women who seek to launch from idea to initiation, grow from initiation to sustainability, or pivot in business to maintain viability or create additional streams of income. The main motivations for these women include a desire for greater independence, challenge, and improved financial opportunity or creativity, which leads to generational wealth, establishment, and implementation of ideas to keep a successful business successful.

I recall a session with a young lady who visited my office, and her words were so touching as she uttered, "I have to make this work." She spoke from the point of desperation, as she sought guidance. There are no magic concepts—it happens with hard work. I have learned throughout my career to ensure that I understand the purpose of the client's business, and that the business owner understands their vision and mission, so they don't have what I call "mission creep." Mission creep is when you do whatever, and there is no focus on business.

As we began to discuss this young lady's business, which is health and wellness, I found that most of what she was doing was great and that she has a steady clientele. Her challenge was pricing. As we outlined her inventory, we listed her costs, time, shipping and handling, and labeling. We determined that if she increased her hourly price by five dollars and charged for shipping and handling, she would see a profit almost immediately. There is a difference in profit for pricing and ensuring that your business has a return on investment. Once we concluded our ninety-minute session, she had a thirty-day plan to implement.

It is important to voice the challenges out loud so one doesn't become overwhelmed with them. It is just like eating a pie: one slice at a time. If I had to describe my path to purpose, it would be supporting women to launch and run a business.

Three key components that describe my purpose include education, goals, and motivation.

Education as Knowledge

Both internal and external factors affect our experience. Internal is what my strengths are and what I am capable of achieving. Internal also pulls from the business owner's skill sets, structural characteristics—how they want the business to be set up and business strategy, how they will achieve outcomes. While the path will vary, having multiple skill sets is critical. How one formulates their idea or concept is necessary because they can visualize what they are creating and where it can be implemented, which involves learning. Learning is both formal and informal. For example, education may include what one has gone to school for, i.e., certifications for business development training, or securing a business coach or mentor. Education also includes skills we have and those we can transfer into our business concepts.

Another aspect of education is external, which is learning what is occurring in the environment that would allow a business idea to manifest and become profitable. External factors are those elements we can't control, but we often examine to assist in making a conscious decision in the direction we may need to go. External factors include the industry in which the firm competes and those who are competing against us in the same industry. For example, if a food chain experiences a reduction in returns because of the consumer's dietary needs, what response will need to be made to remain competitive in the environment? In this instance, the response is influenced by the external market and the understanding of the conditions. This is considered a competitor analysis, what trends are occurring, so vision, mission, and choice of strategy to remain competitive can be determined.

The challenge as a business owner, especially for women, is to manage our resources so we can create core competencies to gain a competitive advantage. As women business owners, we are nurturers. As nurturers, we tend to pay attention to things that are occurring around us, so it is very likely we will be cautious to respond to our external environment; meaning, we will identify internally what we do well, we know what our strengths are, and we know what we can do. The external environment suggests what you might do. Women business owners who take time to learn about the industry and the changes that may occur make informed decisions on the direction they want to steer their business.

Goals

In my discovery of women business owners as they seek to launch, setting goals and creating timelines are critical and influence the trajectory of business growth. It is important to ensure that we connect our personal goals with our business goals. If we enjoy what we do, we will never work a day in our lives. We can't be everything to everyone, and as a business owner we cannot do everything. But if we identify what we do well and turn our passions into a profitable business, that will be half the battle. Devote time to setting realistic goals. Realistic goals can include setting up a simple structure, using leadership skills as transferable skills to manage processes, and improving turnaround for customers. Keep in mind that most businesses fail within the formative years, which has been documented as less than three to five years. For success to last, identify challenges and address them rapidly. But also keep in mind it is about growth.

Motivation

It is said that business owners create a condition to earn one's living. Yes! The goal is to have longevity, and it is important to celebrate small victories. Every client or customer should be celebrated. Every new job you create should be celebrated. Every successful marketing campaign should be celebrated. Joining new networks should be celebrated because those networks are potential new clients, and every milestone you designate in your goals are what motivate you. Even challenges. Yes, even challenges. Challenges are also part of your motivation so you can track what is working and when you need to pivot.

In order to have longevity, you must launch, grow, or pivot. But most importantly, you must finish strong!

 Alyce Herndon is an Army veteran and first-generation female entrepreneur who understands the excitement of starting a sustainable new business. Alyce is currently the Director of Grace Hill Women's Business Center, offering entrepreneurial training and one-on-one counseling. Since becoming Director, she has diligently created topic-specific training and increased counseling to reach an average of 500+ women annually.

Alyce is passionate about providing resources to women business owners, regardless of the stage of their business, and has made it her mission to help position them for growth. She was honored as one of the Top 100 people to know in St. Louis in 2018, received the Melton Lewis Award for Equal Justice by Legal Services of Eastern Missouri, and is the recipient of St. Louis Small Business Monthly's Hall of Fame for Small Businesses in 2019.

Alyce started her own organization, Onyx Business Solutions, to continue her work as a counselor, trainer, and facilitator, assisting women who want to launch, grow, or pivot across industries. Onyx Business Solutions is also an affiliate of Black Dress Circle, which further engages and supports women-owned businesses.

info@onyxbusinesssolutions.com
www.onyxbusinesssolutions.com

www.facebook.com/alyce.herndon
www.linkedin.com/in/alyceherndon/
www.instagram.com/alyceherndon/

Your Most Important Investment: You

I've always been hyperaware of money—not because I grew up either wealthy or poor, but because my parents tried to optimize every dollar. They emigrated from the Philippines to a middle-class suburb of San Francisco, where they worked hard, saved, and raised two educated daughters. When you grow up in a third-world country as my parents did, you realize how important it is to stretch your funds—a lesson my parents ingrained in me. I didn't have a lot of toys. We used to cut out coupons; and in stores, my mom would make me do the math to figure out which items were the better value.

But while my parents were great at saving money, they weren't good at accelerating their wealth. They worked hard but didn't negotiate for raises. In many ways, I'm like my parents—I work hard and save a lot—but over the years, I've learned many lessons about building financial security that eclipsed the ones my parents taught me. For me, figuring out how to build wealth went beyond savings and math to a wider view of education and self-care.

In high school, my geometry teacher held a stock-picking contest. I picked Genentech and came in dead last at the end of the semester. I was embarrassed, but the act of picking a stock and seeing how the value spiked fascinated me. I was hooked. If I'd held onto that Genentech stock and we tallied up the results today, I might well have won the contest.

I was such a responsible student that I started making money as a teenager, with teachers referring me to babysit and tutor throughout my hometown. At the University of California at Berkeley, even though I had a double major, volunteered and was involved in many activities, I still worked for extra income: at a bookstore, in an ophthalmology office, and for a catering company. I was an early adopter of having a side gig and hustling for financial security.

In 1999, I was a twenty-three-year-old living in San Francisco with roommates, struggling to break even every month. The income from my first full-time job out of college barely covered my modest expenses. One morning, I woke up with a bad case of the flu, marinating in perspiration; my blankets and sheets were drenched. Budget-constrained to generic over-the-counter medicine, I vowed to find a better paying job; and once I got it, I promised myself a medicine cabinet full of Advil, Nyquil Cold & Flu, and maximum strength Sudafed. That turn for the worse was a turning point for my life: I needed to make more money to take better care of myself.

Excess

I interviewed with a startup and secured an offer that more than tripled my previous salary. With $3 million in funding, the technology startup built a web-based sales and marketing effectiveness application. Ironically, we were more effective at spending than we were at selling our software. After launching the company, we went on an all-expenses paid cruise to Mexico.

By 2001, I'd been working at the startup for almost three years. Twenty percent bonuses were still kicking in until September 11th, when the dot-com bubble turned into a dot-com bust. We lost several major accounts; the pink slips were distributed; and I had a few good cries in our CEO's office as he promised me his highest recommendation and reference. I felt ill—the same way I'd felt at the drugstore when I was only able to buy generic medicine. Just as I'd vowed then to care for myself financially by getting a new job, I promised never to end up like my defeated CEO, laying off employees because of his fiscal irresponsibility.

Trolling the postings on Monster.com for a permanent position, I also looked to make immediate income. I came across a curious ad on Craigslist. The posting read, "Looking for cute girl to clean my loft."

Intrigued, I responded, "Cute laid-off dot-commer looking to make some money under the table." I'm not sure why "cute" was a job requirement, but I'd make it clear it was just cleaning his apartment.

Corey turned out to be a modern-day Master of the Universe. An options trader for the Pacific Stock Exchange, just like Sherman McCoy straight out of *Bonfire of the Vanities*, he shouted "buy" and "sell" and calculated pricing spreads, but on the West Coast—San Francisco's financial district—instead of Wall Street.

His tri-level loft was new construction, a homeowner's dream: floor-to-ceiling windows, stainless steel appliances, a garage, and three bathrooms—one on each floor. I had never seen such a large, spacious home in the city. When my eyes bulged, he asked with concern, "Oh, no. Do you think my place is too big to clean?"

I shook my head no. It wasn't too big to clean; it was too clean to clean.

Months later, one of Corey's dates chastised me for not cleaning his place well enough. I walked out of Corey's loft that day feeling like I was living Cinderella's fairy-tale life in reverse. Someone my own age was telling me where to mop and scrub.

I quit, tired of the life of excess—first as an employee for a dot-com, then as an overpaid maid. I wanted recession-proof skills, the opportunity for a secure future; and I wanted to know what it was like to work hard again, the way I had as an undergraduate student.

Corey didn't need a maid any more than I needed to be a maid. Back then, the tech world didn't need another dot-com, but everything ultimately unwinds itself. The Pacific Stock Exchange was replaced by an Equinox fitness club. Corey moved back home to Boston to work in the family publishing business. The dot-com boom went bust just as the housing bubble popped. And I found myself huddled in a library of one of the top business schools in the world, studying the economics of it all.

Education

I realized that education was the key to the financial stability I had been seeking, and I learned several lessons, both in business school and out. Education is one of the most important investment decisions we'll make, so prospective students shouldn't fall for a program's marketing tactics. Research salient metrics, including graduation rate, job placement, strength of the alumni network and average starting salary, in addition to the cost (both tuition and foregone earnings). Armed with quantitative research, assess the program qualitatively by talking to alumni: How well did the school prepare them? What would they have done differently? How easy was it to get a job? Securing employment post-graduation is critical.

There are many paths to academic success, but spend your time and money where you can expect a significant return. Don't do something because everyone else is doing it—like going into debt to attend a four-year university. Know all of your options, including taking a gap year, attending community college or vocational school, or working.

Education is much broader than formal schooling. I'm a voracious reader, averaging three books a month. Much can be learned, too, from traveling both domestically and internationally, being open to new experiences and learning from diverse cultures. I'm also a firm believer in therapy, mentoring, retreats and conferences for overall self-improvement. Working with a coach, in particular, has helped me live with intention and accountability. I've learned to perceive negative experiences as growth opportunities, and to shift from being internally focused to strengthening connections to my community.

Instead of paying for formal coaching, ask for mentoring from a friend, colleague, boss or trusted leader. Connect regularly and hold each other accountable. Follow people you admire on social media, subscribe to their blog posts and newsletters. There are many free resources to benefit from.

Accelerating Wealth

I feel rich because I work to keep my expenses low. I embrace a frugal, minimal lifestyle: low housing costs, low child care expenses, no car payment, no makeup, minimal beauty services. I bought a friend's car for $1,500. I wear a Casio watch held together by rubber bands. I've adopted a uniform of all black apparel. Less choice allows me to focus on decisions that are more important to me than fashion. I get drastic when it comes to cutting costs. Don't rely on anyone but yourself for sustained financial support—not your parents, spouse, or employer. Situations change.

I'm able to build wealth by accomplishing a lot in short spurts of time. Even though I have a full-time career, companies regularly contact me about my blog or social media presence to promote their brand. Picking up a side hustle benefits your finances, increases your skills and boosts your confidence.

After saving and hustling, focus on accumulating income-generating assets like stocks, real estate, and ownership equity. I started out investing in real estate by buying a duplex that was less expensive than a single-family home. My family lived in one unit and we rented out the other; the rental income covered the mortgage payment. This continues to be my strategy—investing in real estate with a consistent income stream. If the property goes up in value, great; if not, I'm still making money.

Currently, as an angel investor and partnerships executive, I'm adept at identifying promising entrepreneurs and emerging technologies. Successful founders are passionate. They're never stumped by questions because they're knowledgeable about the technology and business model. My first angel investment was in a company called "Shoot My Travel." I was so impressed by the CEO's pitch, I was compelled to invest. The funding round was oversubscribed because the founders had a clear vision, knew exactly what they needed to accomplish, and also what the challenges were. Their energy and enthusiasm were infectious, which is attractive to potential investors, advisors, customers, and employees.

Philanthropy

The myth is that you have to be rich to be philanthropic; when in reality, wealth is a mindset of sufficiency and abundance. This is the central tenet of the powerful book *The Soul of Money: Transforming Your Relationship with Money and Life* by Lynne Twist. *"Eventually, we came to know ourselves not for what we had or owned, but for what we gave; not for what we accumulated, but for what we allocated."*

There are three things I did when I started working full time: 1) contributed to my 401k, 2) continued to invest in stocks, and 3) donated to charities. I've subscribed to the belief, which was passed down from my Catholic faith and my immigrant parents, that the more you give, the more you receive. Philanthropy comes naturally when you realize that life is abundant, that your resources are sufficient, and that your finances are more than enough. In fact, recent research indicates that giving leads to happiness.

Giving back can come from being brave and telling your truth like Malala Yousafzai, the youngest-ever Nobel Laureate, who spoke up for female education. *The Soul of Money* also describes stories of other brave women who were violated or oppressed—who did everything they could to get to a public platform so they could tell their stories of social injustice.

Takeaways

In a post that appeared in the September 28, 2017 issue of Forbes, Warren Buffett wrote, *"But ultimately, there's one investment that supersedes all others: Invest in yourself. Address whatever you feel your weaknesses are, and do it now."*

Remember that being a smart investor isn't only about money. It's about how you fill your mind, where you spend your time, how you make money, how you invest, and how you give back to your community. You're looking for the best return for your financial security—and your life.

 Catherine Gacad is a Senior Vice President for the Advanced Technology Partnerships Group at Wells Fargo. Her role encompasses collaborating internally with stakeholders across the bank and externally with investors, portfolio companies and large cap companies in technology and telecommunications. Before joining Wells Fargo in 2004, Catherine worked for a tech startup, Cisco Systems, and in private equity.

Catherine graduated with honors from UC Berkeley, and she earned her MBA from the University of Chicago, Booth School of Business. Catherine is a San Francisco Bay Area native who has traveled to 32 countries in six continents. She is a strong proponent of philanthropy and female leadership.

Catherine Gacad is a sought-after speaker, presenting on advancement, networking, branding, innovation, and leadership. With a prestigious academic background and cross-functional experience in large corporate, venture capital, private equity, startup and consulting environments, she can engage with audiences as a keynote speaker, panelist, moderator, or workshop presenter.

cgacad@chicagobooth.edu
www.catherinegacad.com

www.linkedin.com/in/cgacad/
www.twitter.com/cgacad

Four Tenets of Team Building

On several occasions, I've been asked the question: "What one thing are you the most proud of in building this business?" I always answer. "Our team." Over the years, I've learned that the company's most important asset is NOT—contrary to business textbooks—its net profitability, client lists, equipment, or expertise; it's the company's people who deliver the customer service and technical expertise to make the rest of those assets obtain and retain their value. But team building was not an easy lesson for me—or any obsessive-compulsive, non-delegating entrepreneur for that matter—to learn.

My Beginnings

I suppose I have always been surrounded by entrepreneurial personalities in my family members and early mentors. I was raised in Norfolk, NE, the hometown of Johnny Carson and the Hall brothers' first company before they created Hallmark in Kansas City. One grandfather owned a television repair store in Oklahoma; another, a farmer in Nebraska. Both my parents were teachers before my father became an independent sales manager and then a restaurant owner with my mother.

My college education took a few detours, earning a Water Science BS, an MS in Agronomy, and later an MBA. A random conference in Kansas City connected me with an international environmental consulting firm which led me to Kansas City. I spent four years learning about governmental contracting, job profitability, and job costing that led to a position of running a small business. After three years of employment at the small business, I knew what I could do and wanted to do, but equally important, what I did NOT want to do.

Life takes many routes, and they all carry value if you're willing to look for it. While the small business position was overall a negative experience, it introduced me to a client who would become a key business contact for me. In the summer of 2007, this contact and I started discussions about forming our own environmental remediation company, combining my regulatory background and his labor management skills. On October 17, 2007, New Horizons Enterprises, LLC, was born in its first incarnation. I sat in my office, contemplating company assets: a computer, $1,000 in the bank, and a single project. My co-founder wasn't willing to quit his job on that prospect, so I bought out his interests and plugged on.

Fast forward twelve years later and I find myself leading two companies, with offices in two states, annual revenues of over $12 million, and an employee group ranging between 100 to 200 employees at any given time. And it ALL tracks back to our main asset—our TEAM.

Know your weaknesses and hire to plug them.

In the beginning, I was fine handling a small book of business. As projects began to accumulate, however, it became apparent I was spreading myself too thin, performing ALL tasks but none to the quality I expected. Recognizing my budget, I hired an office assistant to handle administrative duties and then a fellow environmental scientist so I could focus on start-up marketing and name-building. The formula worked. In November 2008, we landed a quarter-million-dollar project that enabled me to circle back and hire my original partner as vice president, along with a team of three supervisors to handle the increasing work.

BONUS: ALL of these initial people are still with the company twelve years later!

Build your team around your company's vision and values.

This can be problematic for entrepreneurial companies. Often, we start our businesses based on our personal vision but don't try to identify and articulate that vision. We then encounter philosophical misunderstandings that can build to catastrophic failures. This failure can be avoided by some careful reflection on the business owner's part. The exercise can't be done early enough, as the vision directs the growth of the company.

In my instance, the environmental focus was established. I wanted the BEST environmental remediation services available, in a turnkey fashion, at the best price and with the best customer service. After several attempts, this concept was condensed into the company's current mission and core values.

Our mission statement reads:

"To lead government, commercial and residential clients to cost-effective environmental solutions."

This mission statement plays into our five core values: 1) always question the status quo; 2) make every customer feel like they are your only; 3) be professional, safe, and clean; 4) make every deliverable count; and 5) do what you say, when you say you will do it. This statement and our core values are found throughout the company. It is these fundamentals that guide company decisions. These concepts are also reflected in the company's two adages of Stay In Your Lane and Work On The Big Picture.

Our stay-in-your-lane philosophy was generated after our accountant accused us of "driving on back country roads at interstate speeds." The fast-paced growth of the business and our expanding work resulted in our looking like a colony of disturbed ants. Our stay-in-your-lane motto recognizes that while we are there to SUPPORT one another in case there's a gap, we each must also refrain from barging into another's lane to perform a function they are capable of doing.

Each position in the company bears a job description. Employees are encouraged to know and respect these descriptions and the parameters of their "beginning" and "end." Don't step into someone else's role without a need to do so AND without their consent. This concept was problematic at first; but after repeated questions of "Was this truly your lane," employees began to ask this of themselves. We found, over time, we had developed an organic referral process where work or questions were directed to the person best suited to handle that function.

Our work-on-the-big-picture adage extrapolates from this. On each business decision and project, we analyze the goal of the project against our mission statement and core values. We then attempt to perform each project in alignment with those visions and goals.

BONUS: A clear mission and vision permits your team to recognize and perform their roles to best fulfill the company's current and future vision.

Remember to apply the three "Rs" in team building.

Team building is a slow, brick-by-brick process. It's built on, what I call, the "Three Rs": Recruitment, Reward, and Retention.

Recruitment. Effective recruitment requires a recognition of a company's mission and core values, its services, its clientele, its staffing, and where existing or projected new holes may appear, and then combing the market for candidates to fill in the holes. We've found that, in many instances, our best candidates are entry level and we train them on our ways and beliefs. A willingness to adopt the company's values and the ability to fit into the culture are as valuable as work experience or education. Be creative and don't limit yourself in the recruitment process.

Reward. Let's face it. Today's workforce is complicated. We have the contrasting psychological needs of the first multi-generational workforce ever, i.e. Baby Boomers, GenX'ers, Millennials, etc. The specific reward needs of EACH of these groups differ, but so long as we're looking at a formula of salary/benefits/education/kudos/and non-business-related social interactions, we should be able to cover all bases. Our company addressed this element by first creating and then growing quarterly strategic meetings with our executive and management group. Some of the reward concepts of New Horizons were birthed from these sessions, including:

- "Covering the bases" philosophy permits quality time off. The company executives recognize that on any given day, the absence of a key employee could leave a gap in knowledge that is not acceptable. Thus, the entire management group is committed to constant discussion and interaction on pending projects so that, in the event someone is gone for either vacation, medical, or emergency, other employees can step in to fill the gap. This also removes stress of performance obligations from that employee who is absent and permits the company to adopt a "No contact with the office" rule, allowing vacationers to turn off their office minds, enjoy, and recharge. The best example of this concept in operation occurred when three key people were off on either paid maternity or paternity leave at the same time. By our covering-the-bases-philosophy, no balls were dropped and each employee was permitted to enjoy quality, uninterrupted time with their newborns without interfering office problems.

- Employee recognition programs. The executive group recognized that sometimes a visible pat on the back goes a long way. Towards that end, the group established a recognition program that identifies company employees for their various contributions each year.

- Inter-office chit-chat encouraged. Finally, the company adopted a novel but efficient culture of not only NOT PROHIBITING interoffice chit-chat, but encouraging it. Communication is key to effective functioning of a growing business with many moving parts. The full 360-degree view can only be discovered by frequent in-depth conversations between employees. These random discussions keep team members informed of prospects, potential opportunities, job issues and suggested fixes, or potential areas where covering the base opportunities exist or may arise. This creates an organic response which has worked well for the company.

Retention. Retention is key to our company philosophy. We recognize that replacing people is costly to the company in terms of mistakes, inefficiencies in our internal processes, and the quality of our service. We also recognize that each person plays a key role in the symbiotic function of our company—if paperwork isn't filed correctly, when a governmental agency comes to audit, it could result in fines. No one's job here is "minimal" or "unimportant." Retention is discussed frequently and corporate culture reflects that our employees, as our main asset, are VALUED.

Retention is also reflected in our philosophy that we promote from within. We discuss at interviews our commitment to this policy. If an employee wishes to learn from the "ground up," we will do everything in our power to ensure there is always a ground-up opportunity for them. Employees feel like they are part of a team; that they will be supported and encouraged to grow; that there will not be reprimand but learning experiences from mistakes; and that they will not be knifed in the back at the end of the day.

BONUS: By applying the three Rs of team building—recruitment, reward, and retention—we build a happy and functioning team that views itself as an asset of the company.

Get out of the way. Delegate. Then mean it!

I believe the hardest component of team building by an entrepreneur is the recognition that the world will not end with their absence from the business. "Entrepreneur" and "delegator" are oxymorons in our culture. If we hadn't been a little obsessive-compulsive in our initial vision, would the company ever have been founded? How can we step out of the way and be sure it will continue to function without our obsessive micromanaging that served us so well?

Well, get over yourself, and you'll discover your business not only functions without you, but, in some ways, perhaps functions better when your team steps up to their defined responsibilities and elevated expectations. If you're following a true commitment to building, training, valuing, rewarding, and retaining your team, you'll find them capable and proud to handle their respective obligations.

The added benefit is that with a functioning team, your role becomes more fluid. In a micro sense, you have the comfort of knowing your company can perform in your absence. In a macro sense, the company retains a strong independent sales value at some future point even if you don't go along with it. It's just a win-win situation. So, get out of your own way. Fast.

BONUS: If you can learn to delegate, you'll have time to sit back and admire the business you've created, watching your team members grow along with the business.

As I look back at my beginnings, measured against the size and quality of my current operations, I marvel at the depth, resiliency, and never-ending talent of "our team." Without the Four Tenets of Team Building, my team, I, nor the company, would not be where we are today.

 Stephanie Isaacson is the owner, president and CEO of New Horizons, an environmental solutions firm with offices in Kansas City, MO and Lincoln, NE, with customers nationwide. New Horizons' professionals are experienced in site assessments, asbestos, lead-based paint and mold assessments, green building consulting and project management. Over the course of 12 years, she had grown New Horizons from just one person to over 100 employees, and today Isaacson oversees a team that understands the need for creative problem-solving: a solution that worked last year may not work this year, and Isaacson knows that mental flexibility saves New Horizons time and money.

Isaacson has learned that employees are the most important component of her business: if you take care of your people, she understands, then clients will come. The employee, after all, establishes and maintains client relationships; Isaacson creates a positive and supportive working culture to keep her staff happy and productive.

In 2017, Ms. Isaacson started another company, Pink Roll-Off, LLC. a trash hauling company with a professional approach to disposal of construction debris. Ms. Isaacson lives in Kansas City, MO with her husband, 2 year old daughter, and Ollie the dog.

Stephanie@newhorizons-llc.com
www.newhorizons-llc.com
www.pinkrolloff.com

www.facebook.com/newhorizonsenterprises
www.facebook.com/pinkrolloff
www.linkedin.com/in/stephanie-isaacson

Employee and Entrepreneur

I'm a firm believer in doing what you love. I've loved every job I've had and have left it when I stopped loving it. When I started my journey as an entrepreneur, it was about much more than just owning a business or creating a brand. It was about creating something I would love building and maintaining. From the (many times frustrating) building rehab, to conceptualizing the brand, building the team, and meeting students, I focused on staying true to my mission and making sure I'm always doing what I love.

Let's face it—no one is going to retire from $10 yoga classes. For me, becoming an entrepreneur was never about being financially successfully. It was always about creating something I was passionate about. With Brick City Yoga that passion was revitalizing an old building, creating economically accessible yoga classes, helping instructors build a future, and offering a community gathering space.

All that entrepreneurial advice you've read about doing what you love? It's true.

And that part about your people being your best asset? Totally true. I trust my team with everything I have created. They are truly the foundation of the studio's culture.

Oh, and that part about nothing going as planned, things feeling like they are falling apart left and right, and constantly thinking you have zero control and should give up? What? No one told you that? Me neither.

Whether your journey takes you from employee to entrepreneur or to employee and entrepreneur, here are the top five not so glamorous or unexpected lessons I've learned.

Debt is Definitely a Four Letter Word

Forty-five thousand for windows; $100,000 over budget for living space. Overnight I went from having a building and studio that could be paid off in a few years to having a nearly $500,000 side project.

Yikes.

You must be wondering how this could happen to someone who is meticulously accurate with a checkbook.

I can pinpoint most of it—I didn't receive a grant from the city; I forgot to request the first floor renovation in my construction loan; when I started decorating for the studio, my ideas for the perfect space ended up being more expensive than what I had previously decided I was willing to spend.

Once I realized how far over budget I was, my first call was to my banker, followed by brainstorming ways to cut down the costs of remaining work and moving certain portions of the project into phase 2 and phase 3 categories.

The takeaway:

Owning and operating a business is expensive. It not only takes a ton of money, but time, energy, and other resources. Create your budget. Then double it. Know when to cut and when to spend. When starting out, look at all possible funding sources—loans, personal assets, crowd funding, private equity, etc.—and choose the option or options best for you.

Human Resources is More than Being a People Person

I had to fire a yoga instructor. I had known her for years, considered her a friend, and opened my doors to her in more ways than I have words for here. I trusted her. She didn't follow our policies as well as the other instructors, she wasn't engaged in our community at all, and she didn't necessarily support the other instructors. But she was my friend and I trusted her, so I looked past all of the things that may have caught my eye had it been somebody else. Then, I found out she was stealing from me. That was it—I had to let her go. I knew she'd understand and apologize or try to offer an explanation. She didn't—she acted entitled, was not remorseful, and texted me with why what she did was okay. She made me feel guilty for catching her and holding her accountable.

In my years of people management, I have never felt so conflicted about terminating someone who was in the wrong. I couldn't seem to separate work from personal and it took weeks for me to come to accept that this person was okay breaking my trust and walking away from a relationship.

The takeaway:

It's okay to take things personally. As business owners, and especially as women, we often hear to keep business and personal separate, but when the business is yours, it can and should be personal. You can't prevent yourself from taking an employee loss personally, but you can arm yourself with solid policies and processes to guide you. Keep a trusted employment attorney on speed dial for the answers to questions you shouldn't Google.

Not All PR is Good PR

I woke up to several Facebook and Instagram notifications— friends and students wanting to make sure everything was okay. I couldn't figure out why until I saw the studio tagged in our neighborhood Facebook group. A local news station had broadcast with our windows as a backdrop during the 5pm, 10pm and subsequent 6am broadcast. My attempts to reason with the reporter were futile and followed by class and workshop cancelations.

Only open a few months, I certainly hadn't planned on needing a PR response. With no options to change the story, I shared the following statement with our community:

"This week a neighbor in the BPW Facebook group posted an image from his home security system. His caption stated someone in the car was shooting from the sunroof. He asked neighbors to check their footage. A neighbor mentioned Brick City Yoga. I checked our cameras and replied that while we had the time requested from multiple angles, we did not show any crimes being committed.

The original poster asked for our footage. I stated we would not post because no crime was committed, and we are not responsible for enforcing any laws or passing judgment. I also stated I would not provide him with the footage, only to law enforcement if there was a police report. His response was there was not.

KMOV Channel 4 contacted him through the thread. The reporter was able to see my comments as the studio owner. They ran the story in a misleading way broadcasting with the studio as the background. According to KMOV, the "anonymous neighbor" requested the location. They also stated since they used the words "near" not "at" they were within broadcasting standards and did not need to issue a correction.

Is this true? Most likely. Some pretty great attorneys are checking for me though. Ultimately, it's irresponsible and misleading "journalism" that at best can be a scare tactic and at worse a cheap click bait attempt.

I know there is crime everywhere. My instructors and our students know that too. Was there a crime committed on the 2900 block of Wyoming this week? I don't know that with 100% certainty and it's not my job to prove or disprove. I can tell you there wasn't one committed at 2758.

What I can tell you is that our studio is committed to the neighborhood. We are accessible to everyone, we are affordable, and we give back when we can. I have personally invested a ton of money into the building and landscaping to improve the corner for our neighbors. We added very high tech and visible cameras to increase safety and deter crime. You know what—it seems to be working.

I know how committed the neighborhood association is to improving the community. It's disappointing to see neighbors and outsiders discourage this type of effort or frame it in a way that implies they are ignorant of anything negative.

Sensationalized "journalism" does not help neighborhoods trying to do better. The story had an immediate, negative and financial impact on our studio. I imagine it had or has the potential to do the same to other hard-working families in the neighborhood.

I hope our students feel safe in the studio, I hope they understand this piece was a scare tactic, and I hope our neighbors find more value in creating sustainable change than they do in a media moment."

The takeaway:

You will never be fully prepared for negative PR when a situation is totally out of your control. Plan for what you can. And for everything else that comes at you—be honest, be authentic, and stay true to your brand values.

Community is Key

Puppies! The studio was full of yogis, a local brewery was sampling drinks, and some adorable pit bull mixes were running around.

When I started the studio, I had four main goals: offer economically accessible yoga, make everyone feel welcome, offer instructors an opportunity to create earning potential, and give back to the community.

Since the studio's opening, we've chosen one charity per month to support. Some months, this is donating a portion of class revenue back to the charity and some months its hosting dedicated events to support a chosen charity.

We choose local charities that have a connection with an instructor, a student or the immediate neighborhood. As a startup, we aren't always able to give a lot, but we always strive to show gratitude to a community that welcomed us.

The takeaway:

You are inherently a part of your community. Make it better than how you found it. Whether you can give a little or a lot, the impact will go much farther than just a social media plug.

Sometimes Flexibility is More Important Off the Mat

I was 1.5 hours away from the city. I had over 5 missed calls from my upstairs tenant. A missed call from my instructor. And then an emergency text from my general contractor.

Two distracted drivers had crashed into the building during a yoga class.

By the time I got back to the studio, the damage was worse than I expected. Well, maybe not. I mean, a car drives through your building and you expect it to be pretty bad, right? But the damage was real. For 90 minutes I convinced myself everyone else was over-reacting. They weren't. Turns out they were trying to keep me from worrying too much.

An instructor was in the hospital getting stitched up, a student had scrapes from glass, the windows were shattered, blood was all over the floor and emergency crews warned us about structural damage.

We closed for a day. The instructors wanted to teach and students wanted to take classes, so we opened that weekend and the community showed up in a big way.

The following week I started the process of meeting with adjusters, contractors, inspectors, engineers and lawyers. It's a process I'm still going through as I write this, but I know we will rebuild and be as good as new by the time this book is published.

The takeaway:

Sometimes a car can literally (or figuratively) drive through what you've built. When it happens, be flexible. Know your patience will be tested. But also know, if you are an entrepreneur because you truly love what you do, whom you work with and the people you serve—you will move forward.

Oh, and make sure you have a killer insurance policy.

*****

If you are reading this chapter, the studio has, hopefully, just finished our one-year anniversary celebration. That's right—all those stories you read happened before we turned one.

I hope your journey is just as rewarding, and perhaps a little less exciting. And, to see how we're doing now, follow us at brickcityyogastl.com.

Kate Ewing is a results-oriented strategic marketing professional. She currently serves as the Director of Strategic Business Development and Marketing for the St. Louis-based law firm, Sandberg Phoenix, where her primary focus is to drive business results through developing and implementing marketing, communications, and business development strategies for the firm.

As a certified yoga instructor, Kate strives to take her practice from the mat to the office daily. Outside of work, Kate serves on several local charitable boards and committees, with an emphasis on cancer research funding, arts and education, and re-entry services. She also mentors female entrepreneurs in several areas including securing funding, creating business plans and implementing marketing strategies.

In 2018, Kate began her journey to entrepreneurship with the purchase and renovation of the building that would later become Brick City Yoga.

Kate is a St. Louis native who currently lives in the St. Louis Tower Grove East neighborhood with her rescue cats and is aunt to her sister's kids, Aiden, Zoey and Julia.

kate.d.ewing@gmail.com
www.brickcityyogastl.com

www.linkedin.com/in/kateewing
www.instagram.com/brickcityyogastl/

Lead Up for Women

Enduring weekly abuse was easier to heal than the words he spoke that day. "She's not worth one hundred dollars per month," he stated. Those were the last words I remember hearing my dad say as he packed up his every belonging to head across country to embark on the next chapter in his life. I was the youngest of three children in my family. We were what I would refer to as "a normal family"! We would go to church on Sunday, spend evenings with homework and favorite weekly television shows, and spend the summers in Utah with my aunt and grandparents. Camping was a regular activity, and life seemed the same compared to my friends' upbringings. It wasn't until I was an adult that I realized how different we really were. I guess it was a blessing in disguise that my dad left when I was twelve years old. That very day, I became responsible for the rest of my life. Even though it was too early to grow up and take on the responsibilities of those twice my age, there wasn't a proposal for any other life path to be had. And so it shall be. The path was marked, and it was up to me to start my journey.

At the age of thirty-six, I was yet again, a single mother. Is this what life is all about? Looking for the next true love? Failing to endure another marriage or painful relationship? It was in this moment I realized that if I was in control of my actions and my story, then why did life suck so badly? Why was it so hard for me to have the fairy-tale love that we dream about as girls? Or did I not dream about that as a girl? I couldn't even remember what my dreams were at this point. Who and what was I chasing all of these years? When I hit rock bottom, I knew it was time to flush out the pain the hurt and the yet-to-be uncovered. Hello therapy!

It was me I had been chasing and I didn't even know it. Crazy to think that up to this point in my life, I thought that the daily miles I ran, weekly visits to the gym, yoga classes, and annual marathons were all the therapy I needed. Well, I was wrong! It took the right person, at the right time to help me unlock the cage that I had placed myself in. I needed someone outside my frame to show me that the handle was on the inside the entire time. I needed to turn the handle so I could come out of the shadows. I call this time of my life "the awakening"! I literally woke up, as if I had been living in a life of complete darkness. I was able to see my childhood for exactly what it was. I was able to face those that I allowed to carve out my path and forgive those that wronged me. It was a pivotal point in my life to clear out the hurt, the pain, the self-doubt, and to transform my thoughts to attract the life that God intended for me.

My new-found vulnerability allowed my heart to open for the first time and welcome my soulmate. I'm happy to share: We have been married for eleven years. This step to understanding what it was like to truly feel support, equality, and love was the catalyst to the next chapter in my journey to lift those around me.

My years in corporate America seemed to be the right fit as I climbed the ladder to executive leadership. Coaching CEOs through the launch of their businesses and beyond fueled my drive for excellence. I mastered servant leadership and shared my knowledge with everyone I came in contact with. I took on anything and everything within my work and my personal life that involved giving back through service. My heart was filled with gratitude for this opportunity to fulfill my leadership opportunities. I even achieved a first degree in the practice of Taekwondo. Yet, there was still something missing. Que Self-Discovery 2.0!

I traveled eighty percent of each month during my last twenty-four months with my corporate position. Spending several hours at a time in a car or plane was not uncommon, so I took to listening and learning the audible way. Have you ever felt you were meant for something more? That your intuition was telling you to pioneer your own path? These were the continuous thoughts as I navigated my way through forty-eight states. Each visit with clients, every discussion, brought me closer to my destiny. People. Stories. Community. Showing Up. Validation. Confidence. Bingo! This is why I'm here! My mind erupted like a volcano with visions, thoughts, ideas, and plans that were so vivid—even today, I'm overwhelmed by the thought of the clarity I was offered in that very moment. The seeds were planted!

Fast forward six months to the ah-ha moment. I was attending a retreat for women in the commercial construction industry for business development. I had attended once before in the past, but this time it was different. Without the weight of the cage I had previously been standing within, I was able to clearly see, as if the optometrist had handed me glasses for the first time, how each woman possessed her own unique power in her approach to her position. The power in the room felt like static electricity. The sense of support they each shared for their fellow sisters and the thread of connection for the understanding of how difficult it can be for women in this industry was astounding. Was it really only for women in the construction industry?

Heck no! It was for all women! Women in IT, healthcare, finance and every other industry of business. "I'm going to change the world" were the words I whispered when the roundtable session ended. I walked right up to my friend, who ran the retreat and is now my business partner, and said, "We can do this bigger and change more lives." Get this: He's a man and his name is David Corson! He is the perfect man for this organization because of his unwavering support for women and his unique connection model and approach that lends itself to every industry. The journey to empower women to show up and lean into their purpose began! You see, that day, in that room, every woman showed up! They felt safe in the community, let down their guard for a moment and became vulnerable with others. When women are together in a community, they do not succumb to hierarchy; instead, they simply support and connect. Change begins here!

The business-plan building began the week after the event in August of 2018. Just a short four months later, Lead Up for Women was launched.

During those four months, we walked purposefully through the branding process to create a vision and mission, and to determine our core values. This is essential when launching a business as you need to ensure you have the correct messaging and are presenting a solution to a problem that exists in the world today. Women not showing up as themselves and unleashing their power is a problem and the platforms that Lead Up for Women offers are the solution.

We created a partnership with an attorney, outlined a brand and logo when working through the brand process, launched a website, opened a bank account, and prepared for the marketing campaign we had built to launch to women of every ethnicity, culture, and age come January 2019. I know in my heart that, as women, we tend to lose ourselves to our many identities; and it's time to get her back! It's amazing that we even know what our favorite color is or what food we enjoy by the time our kids graduate college. As women in history have pioneered for change, we too must take on the responsibility to pioneer the future for our daughters and granddaughters. This approach to Lead Up for Women is through community and support for each of us to realize our greatest potential.

I couldn't resist the temptation when VoiceAmerica asked us to lead their Women's Series that they were launching on the Empowerment Channel. I stayed up night after night listening to podcasts, researching how to interview, what to ask, what not to say, who to invite on the show, how to market, and everything else you can imagine it would take to be a successful radio show host. After a month, with a binder full of notes, I felt prepared enough to step into the studio.

With over 3.4 million listeners, the majority of them women, I knew Lead Up for Women had to hit the radio waves. I'll be honest. Being a radio show host was never on my mind and was not a vision I had for Lead Up. At the time we were offered the show, I was still working at corporate, traveling for business, launching our first edition of "Lead Up for Women" magazine, launching our luncheon series across the nation; and I was teaching fitness classes weekly in my local community. Yet, it was the right time and another platform which allowed us to share women's stories. These stories inspire and motivate our global listeners. It gives them the permission they seek and need to tap into their super-power and lean into their purpose, write their stories, and fulfill their dreams. How grateful I am to the amazing women I have had the pleasure of interviewing and will interview in the future.

Having the energy to endure many projects at once and to show up as me, each time and in every situation, is my superpower. I see others for exactly who they are, without judgment, good and bad. I didn't always realize that was my superpower, but just as a pearl is born from a grain of sand, I too was "born" from the grit that entered my world. Showing up for women and having the events platform is certainly one of my favorite legs of Lead Up! In 2019, we planned luncheons in a different city, every month, across the nation. We would create the event on our website about four weeks prior, market through social media and Eventbrite, organize local panelists, and send out a newsletter invite.

David and I are personal connecters. Over the past twenty years or so, we have nurtured and grown our contact lists. Doing this for so many years proved to be the catalyst and foundation for a successful launch. We reach out to individuals regularly and personally invite our contacts to our events through phone calls, LinkedIn invites, personal emails, and text messages. If you don't have a strong contact list, I would recommend creating one. I talk to everyone I meet for two reasons: to learn their story and to gather their contact information to see how I can assist them in connecting with the thousands of contacts I know. When your mission is to change the world, one person at a time, you look for every opportunity to do so, even on a plane. So, the next time you are on a plane or have the opportunity, see who you can connect with; it just might change your life and theirs, forever!

The journey with Lead Up for Women has been more gratifying than I ever imagined. Women all over the world connect with us through our online mediums and radio. They receive our newsletters, comment on our website, submit and read articles for the bi-monthly magazine, and have become part of a community of women that lift, support, accept, contribute, endorse, and love one another. There is a plethora of reasons to support why it's impossible to create change in this world, especially from a child that believed she was not worth one hundred dollars per month. An initiative begins with one person, one idea. One person believing in herself. Momentum begins from within. Find the handle. Turn the handle. Believe in you and believe it's possible, and you too can pick up the pen and write your story. Your future is waiting.

Colleen Biggs recently launched Lead Up for Women, an elite community of like-minded women driven by passion, power and purpose. She teaches that in order to be, have, and do anything in life you desire, you must first Gain Clarity! She travels the nation hosting powerful retreats which empower, motivate, and educate women to #leadwithoutpermission.

Colleen believes that life is about thriving—not simply surviving. As a survivor of early childhood chaos, loss, and abuse, Colleen realized the power of community and gained the clarity to understand the magnitude of loving others unconditionally. An inspiration to others, Colleen now helps women realize their worth, gain clarity, and SHOW UP.

Her over 30 years of successful experience in corporate America includes coaching over 300 CEOs, franchising, and launching numerous projects. Her volunteer work includes organizing local and national retreats for women and girls, serving as a director for her church, as well as on several advisory boards.

Colleen has a weekly radio show, Speak Up to Lead Up, on Voiceamerica® Empowerment Channel, and publishes a bi-monthly magazine. She is happily married to the love of her life with seven children and nine grandchildren.

colleenb@leadupforwomen.com
www.leadupforwomen.com

www.facebook.com/leadupforwomen
www.twitter.com/LeadUpforWomen
www.linkedin.com/in/colleen-biggs-3a22a45/
www.instagram.com/leadupforwomen/

Diana George

A Company Culture
that Transforms

It was supposed to be a temporary job that I had found posted on none other than Craigslist. Their current Human Resources manager was on maternity leave and the first temp they had hired found a permanent position. At my first interview, I met the vice president of Human Resources and we hit it off right away. She was engaging, smiling, and genuinely happy. Everyone that I met in this workplace was just as happy. The staff smiled and there seemed to be a positive energy as people went about their day. What impressed me the most was the number of employees that I would come in contact with that had been with the company many years. I met people with tenure from fifteen to twenty to thirty-five years—and they were truly happy to be there. The company culture was calling me, and I was ready to work there. I was offered the job even though I was told I was overqualified. I jumped in, excited to take on the challenge. I became the temporary Human Resources manager of a retail division that, at the time, had twenty-two stores throughout the United States. Twenty-two stores meant twenty-two store managers. I felt I needed to implement an immediate strategy for gaining their confidence and support.

1. My first strategy: listen.

During my first week at the company I called each store manager to introduce myself and to ask what I could do to help them. The results were amazing. People felt heard and they started sharing their thoughts. Andy Staley a widely popular pastor and author of the book, *The Next Generation Leader* said, "Leaders who don't listen will eventually be surrounded by people who have nothing to say."

When employees feel listened to, they feel that their contributions make a difference. They feel part of something larger than themselves; they feel part of a group.

2. My second strategy: set standards and expectations for employee participation.

The Brand division consisted of a small group of five individuals. We were supposed to have weekly division planning meetings. The first week I showed up at the designated meeting place, at the appointed time, but the time came and went and I was the only person there. Week after week, I would continue to show up, even if I was the only person there. Eventually, other people started showing up until we had the entire division showing up weekly.

The turning point was the day we were all at the meeting and the brand president walked by and asked what we were doing. In what would become the norm, he then joined us for our weekly meetings thereafter.

The creativity that comes from individuals in this type of environment—one which sets standards and expects participation—has led to some of the most innovative products and successful companies such as Hilton, Salesforce, American Express and

HubSpot. All companies on the 2019 Fortune 100 Best Companies to Work For list.

3. My third strategy: identify qualities and skill sets.

Our Human Resources division was part of a parent company which had eighteen brands and a company culture that had been created over a period of time. The challenge for me as the Human Resources Director was to take that company culture and infuse it into our brand. A brand widely known for its product but just starting their retail division in the United States. In order to do that successfully, we had to know who we were and what we were trying to do as a company. This was not only for our external customers, but our internal customers (our employees) as well.

When I arrived, I noticed the company had been hiring people from other recognized companies with the thought they would be successful in our company, yet that was NOT the case. The organization had failed to identify who the ideal employee was for our company and culture, and with that came growing pains. I stepped back and thought about the goals, qualities, and skill sets that would help us reach those goals. I came up with our ideal candidate. With this we had a winning formula. As an organization we went from being unknown in our industry to being the place that people wanted to work. Having a group of individuals who share the same purpose on a daily basis is invaluable.

4. My fourth strategy: create a family environment so employees feel connected.

In the fall of 2012, Hurricane Sandy hit and paralyzed parts of New Jersey creating major impacts on our corporate office. We were closed for over a week. Many employees were affected: some lost electricity, some needed roads that were shut down, and some were even rescued from flooding. As we started returning to work, it became apparent that it would take more than a week to get back to normal. For some employees who still lacked electricity, work was a place that gave them stability during the course of the day. The company, recognizing this, catered and provided lunch every day for the next week.

Our Human Resources Department convened to find out which employees were affected and how, as a company, we could help during this difficult time. According to Workhuman.com, 52% of us spend more than 30 hours a week with family compared to 91% who spend the same amount of time with colleagues. We spend more time with our co-workers than with our partners, our kids, and ourselves. It was the experience of taking care of colleagues that led us to start a volunteer group, which I chaired. Our first initiative was a winter-clothing drive and we chose a local organization who would benefit. All the employees had a personal connection to the cause and it showed. The response from the receiving organization was overwhelming when we presented them with one of their largest donations ever.

5. My fifth strategy: exemplify work-life integration from the top down.

It has been called many things: work-life balance or work-life integration, among others. Jeff Bezos, Chief Executive Officer of Amazon, calls it work-life harmony. Whatever you call it, the pursuit of balance as part of the company culture, as practiced from the top down, is essential.

A great example of this is when the brand president that I worked for made certain his family knew they were a priority. He had two daughters who were very young; the oldest, in elementary school. We would often be in a meeting when his daughters got home from school and the oldest would call her dad. It didn't matter what we were doing, he would always take her call, let her know he was in a meeting, and tell her he would call her back.

I knew something was wrong when my stepdad called me. He wanted to know if I had spoken to my mom. When I did eventually speak with my mom, I learned she was to have open heart surgery and wanted me to be there with her in Jacksonville, Florida. Because I worked for a company that valued family, I didn't have to worry. I immediately made the arrangements and was with her prior to the surgery and until she returned home from the hospital. The company culture supported these types of decisions and I was practicing the behavior I wanted from my immediate staff and others in our organization.

Setting the example for work-life harmony has to start at the top. Some people have said that workers should separate their personal lives and their work lives. It's not possible, and it doesn't allow for the human element that we all need that makes us truly our best. In my human resources world, I have seen people at their worst and at their best. I have been there for births, deaths, marriages, divorces, demotions, promotions, and retirements. It is all a part of life and having a culture which recognizes this is healthy. Parents would proudly send me pictures of their newborns, which I hung on my "Employees of the Future" office wall. This was clear proof that life existed outside of work, and an important life event that needed to be shared at work.

Demonstrating work-life integration at the top gives employees the example to do the same thing in their own lives. Some people think that, as a result, though, you would get employees that take advantage. I'm not going to say that never happens, but what I can say is that the overall majority of employees are fully committed to doing their best.

In my career I have been very fortunate to work for some amazing companies with cultures that bring out the best in people. The truth is, it took me a while to discover that not all companies operate this same way. Because of this, I have taken chances, stepped up and out of my comfort zone to do things I have never done before. It has given me opportunities for growth, not only in my professional life but my personal life as well. A close friend of mine just recently said that I am fearless in taking on new endeavors. I say that the previous companies that I have worked for made it safe for me to do so.

6. **My sixth (and best) strategy: create a culture where the company purpose is driven forward by its employees.**

In the fall of 2011, I made the decision to get a part-time job at our stadium working the football season. What most people don't realize is, for a Sunday night football game, the staff arrives around 1:00 p.m. I had gone through the training and I was ready for my first game. I soon realized the training didn't prepare me for what the company expected. I didn't get home until 5:00 a.m. the next morning. As we checked out at the end of the night, or should I say morning, I heard employees complaining. Needless to say, in my head, I thought, "I will never do this again!" The company had stressed in its training that the customer experience was of utmost importance; unfortunately, they failed to give employees a great experience.

After some contemplation, I wrote a letter to the corporate office. Not only did I get a return call, but I was also pulled in by the operation manager on the local level. He wanted to know about my experience. As a result of this, he decided to put together a focus group of employees to see how conditions could be improved. Now that's listening and improving your company culture. I stayed with them several seasons, even working Super Bowl XLVIII where Bruno Mars headlined the half-time show.

Work is fundamental and part of our existence, but how many people return from work every day unfulfilled? That's when work becomes a job that, too often, we dread. Too often, if employees look like they're having a good time at work, it is perceived as "not working" or "not getting things done." Just the opposite: Work should be fun and employees should be happy to go to work. My definition of a career is something that I enjoy doing, that I pop up out of bed to go to work, excited for the challenge.

7. My seventh strategy: pay it forward.

I was fortunate that I knew the type of company culture that I wanted to be involved with. Many people don't take a look at this before they accept a position. It was this that prompted me to go into human resources. I have had the good fortune to impact and bring out the best in people every day. More importantly, I have been able to create a career for myself that I love and I am passionate about. Everywhere I go, people ask me how I connect to people so easily. Well, I like people and believe that everyone has *something* that they are good at; and if you can pull this out of them, you have a jewel in your company. A healthy, positive company culture will do just that. My track record with positive company cultures has allowed me to share what I have learned with others and with you.

"Being a great place to work is the difference between being a good company and a great company."

–Brian Kristofek
President & CEO, Upshot

 As the founder and president of By George HR Solutions, Diana George brings with her a wealth of experience. Her previous leadership roles with global companies such as BOSE and the Swatch Group (specifically their luxury brand OMEGA) prepared her to pull together winning teams for her clients. In addition to providing Management Consulting for small business owners, Diana's ability to handle Human Resource issues for her clients became an added bonus and proved to be a positive contribution to her clients' overall success.

Diana maintains that integrity is the most vital and strongest trait of any organization. With over three decades experience in a career encompassing leadership in retail, non-profit, health and wellness, and the private sector, Diana learned very early on how important integrity and ethics are in the success of any business.

Diana also observed that in the most successful businesses people worked together as a team. Management not only ran those teams but if needed would step in and help at the ground level. Diana uses this same approach as she works with companies to realize and strengthen the resources they have in their employees.

diana@bygeorgehr.com
www.bygeorgehr.com

www.linkedin.com/in/dianalgeorge/
www.facebook.com/ByGeorgeHR/
www.twitter.com/ByGeorgeHR
www.instagram.com/bygeorgehr/

Roberta Moore

ACE Your EQ

I am a person who has successfully recovered from having a low EQ strategy. Now, I teach others how to improve theirs. You may or may not be familiar with your EQ. In the EQ-i 2.0 model, emotional intelligence (EQ) is defined as: a set of emotional and social skills that influence the way we perceive and express ourselves, develop and maintain social relationships, cope with challenges, and use emotional information in an effective and meaningful way.

There are many different elements to emotional intelligence. Several well-known researchers have concerned themselves with how emotional thought contributes to logical thought and affects both our personal, professional and integrated lives. Howard Gardner of Harvard University was the first to write about "multiple intelligences" and what he called personal intelligence, or the ability of introspection. Dr. Reuven Bar-On was the first to use the phrase emotional quotient, or EQ. John Mayer of the University of New Hampshire and Peter Salovey of Yale University were the first to coin the phrase emotional intelligence, or EI.

Dr. Steven Stein founded MHS (Multi-Health Systems) and paved the way to publish, distribute and process Dr. Reuven Bar-On's assessment, the EQ-i 2.0. Bar-On had studied EQ since the 1980's in an effort to understand the answer to two basic questions: what makes people successful and what makes people happy? Like Drs. Stein and Bar-On, I am fascinated by the progress that can be made when we focus on the positive instead of the negative.

According to scientifically valid and reliable data collected from the EQ-i 2.0, anyone at any age can improve their EQ by doing cognitive-behavioral exercises. This is an inspiring and optimistic discovery!

When I stumbled upon these findings, I was a Licensed Marriage and Family Therapist with a flourishing private practice in North Carolina. I was noticing that professionals who came to me seeking help for personal problems almost always needed help with their careers. For example, if they were having trouble communicating with their spouse or loved one, we would discover they were likewise having trouble communicating clearly with a boss or direct report.

I was looking for a way to bring family systems theory into the workplace without a stigma. This meant that instead of giving corporate organizations, executives and managers a mental health diagnosis (which can be stigmatizing) I could offer them an EQ assessment/diagnosis (which would not be). In addition, the professional leader could receive a numerical score and see how they rank according to a sizeable database (or norm group) of other professionals. We could create a developmental plan based on the assessment results to build critical skills through one-on-one or even group coaching. In as few as six months later, we could administer the assessment again to evaluate their progress! Most people are excited by seeing concrete, numerical evidence of how they increased their EQ.

In order to become certified in this tool, I had to assess myself. You might think that because I had been in successful private practice for twelve years at that point, steadily seeing a constant forty clients per week that I would have scored high in the EQ skills necessary for entrepreneurship. You can imagine my upset when I found out I only scored adequately, or in the medium range.

This initial upset turned out to be a blessing in disguise because it propelled me into greater consciousness. I started thinking that if I had done reasonably well with only adequate EQ skills; imagine what I could do with high ones! I got to work and hired an executive coach trained exclusively in the EQ-i 2.0. Together we focused on building my confidence and assertiveness skills (I already had very high empathy). One of the most life-altering exercises was doing "mirror work": looking at myself in the mirror while reciting a litany of my most robust accomplishments. This built my self-esteem and in turn helped me be more pro-active and take necessary actions. I learned to voice my opinions in a direct way even when they might be unpopular or not well-received and stand up for myself. Having the coach validate my progress changed my career and personal life. Having higher EQ helped me move my business to a different state while retaining 33% of my clients and also rebranding or expanding service offerings. I achieved higher productivity, profitability, and personal fulfillment. This is why I am so passionate about it and an avid champion of helping people build their EQ skills.

Let's look at how emotional intelligence is defined.

Digging into this concept, I suspect you can easily relate to why these skillsets would be important to your success. As women business owners, who among us hasn't had to use our influence with our clients and customers in a positive way? Or cope with challenges like too many deadlines and not enough time to complete them? What about building sustainable relationships with clients or key customers, staff or direct reports? And who doesn't want a meaningful and effective personal life?

You may find it easy to understand that to be an effective leader which includes entrepreneurs who are in fact leaders, you would want to ACE your emotional intelligence: meaning have a high level of assertiveness, confidence, and empathy. You may imagine that most leaders and entrepreneurs would score high in these, but in truth, not all do as my story would attest. In the spring of 2013, I scored low in assertiveness, medium in confidence and really high (thankfully!) in Empathy.

Confidence or Self-Regard is defined as being able to like and accept yourself, warts, farts, bumps, bruises and all. Assertiveness is your ability to take action and have initiative; and to negotiate win-win contracts or agreements. Empathy is the ability to put yourself in someone else's shoes and see things from their point of view so that the other person will feel seen, heard, and understood. I believe I was unusual, because in my experience of working with leaders, entrepreneurs and business owners, I find that most score higher in confidence and assertiveness and much lower in empathy than I did.

Let's assume I'm right and that you don't really have to work on your confidence or assertiveness, but you think you are a little shaky in your empathy skills. How would you know and what does that mean? Let's start by looking at your answers to these two questions: When you encounter a person who has a viewpoint different than your own, do you put yourself in their shoes and attempt to understand it? Do you consider what kinds of experiences they have had that might be different from yours that led to the formation of how they see the world? How you answer these two questions contributes to how understood, valued, or acknowledged a person may feel in your presence.

As you might guess, developing your empathy helps you divert your unconscious bias and fosters diversity and inclusion, so it is critical to your entrepreneurial success. Without it, clients or customers, and key staff employees may leave your business or seek products and services where they feel more welcome and appreciated.

Now that you understand how important empathy is, how do you develop yours if you find it lacking? Here are five different strategies:

1. Start with a friend. Have a conversation with them and listen intently. Focus 100% of your attention on them without interruption. When they are finished speaking, tell them everything you heard them say. Now ask them if you got it right. Continue repeating what you heard or asking questions until you are both certain you heard and understood accurately.

2. Ask them if you were a good listener.

3. In the exercise above, make sure to refrain from expressing your own viewpoints or judgements. Leave your own perspective out of it and don't tell your friend that they are right or wrong because this is simply a listening and acknowledging exercise.

4. Take a self-inventory. How much time do you spend focusing on other people vs. on yourself? Aim for a good balance of 50/50.

5. How well do you know your best friend, partner, or employee? Do you know what is really important to them? Ask and find out.

Let me tell you a story about Adele. Adele was a client of mine that self-reported as very low in empathy after taking the EQ-i 2.0 assessment. Adele owned a commercial real estate business and her lack of this important EQ skill was causing her to lose important clients and business deals. Her employees were not productive and only did the bare minimum. Every day Adele was leaving money on the table due to lost opportunity.

As sometimes happens when people have low empathy, Adele did not believe her assessment results. It took six months of working together before she started to see and understand how her cold demeanor was impacting her employees, clients, and business partners. Adele would bring me stories of how a deal failed, and I would point out to her why her lack of empathy was a major part of her derailment.

Once she accepted this as truth, she rolled up her sleeves and got to work. I asked her to keep a mood journal. Three times a day, at 8:00 a.m., noon, and 5:00 p.m., I asked her to stop what she was doing and "report in" to her journal. She listed what she was doing or working on, what she was feeling, and whether the work involved other people. If it did, I asked her to list what the other person(s) was probably feeling. After she got used to keeping this record for about a month, I asked her to add one more item: what was the other person really feeling after she asked them directly. This made it easier for us to look into any patterns that may be contributing (either positive or negative) to her communication style relative to her mood.

After some time, we identified a few patterns. Mostly, she noticed that whenever she was involved in work she didn't like or found boring, her focus was on herself, she was irritable, and she almost always lacked empathy for any other person involved. Next, when she began asking people what they really felt, she found that her reality testing was really off balance and her guess was often wrong. That was a big wake-up call for her and after learning this she doubled-down on her journaling and did even more that what I requested.

When she became genuinely motivated to learn more about the people in her life: what their priorities were, what they cared about, and how they felt, her feelings towards them started to change. As her empathy skills started to bloom, she began to make an internal shift in her attitude. As a result, she reported fewer instances of being bored at work because learning about people and their feelings became more interesting to her. Her employees became more engaged in their work because they felt valued and cared for. Her clients felt acknowledged and understood so she won more business deals.

Adele and her team became more productive, profitable, and personally fulfilled! This was a direct result of the power of increasing her EQ score. When we re-assessed her at the end of the engagement, she scored within the top leadership norms on assertiveness, confidence, and empathy (you can remember this as ACE). These are three EQ skills that in my experience make a critical difference for business success.

No matter how many times you've tried to learn to use your emotions to motivate yourself in a positive direction and failed, don't stop making the effort! Remember, anyone at any age can increase their EQ by doing cognitive-behavioral exercises. Learning to express, manage, control, and contain your emotions is not like flipping a light switch: it doesn't happen overnight. If you persist in trying, you will make small gains over time that add up to a giant leap forward! For instance, I worked with an EQ coach consistently for over two years. Recently, I had the occasion to take the EQi-2.0 assessment again as a requirement for advanced training in leadership development and change navigation. Words cannot fully express my joy at discovering I had scored (meaning how I compared to the norm of other professionals) ~~was~~ within the top 1%. Knowing where I came from, the hard work I did, and where I am now gives me a solid feeling of confidence and assuredness. I wish the same for you!

 Roberta Moore, founder of EQ-i Coach and author of *Emotion at Work: Unleashing the Secret Power of Emotional Intelligence,* utilizes her extensive background as an accomplished business executive and licensed therapist to help executives, business teams, and sales teams achieve workplace and personal success.

In her almost two decades as an individual and family therapist, Moore learned that the key skills responsible for successful personal relationships are the same ones that spark workplace success. With this discovery, Moore has been able to help companies succeed by focusing on emotional and cognitive intelligence behaviors and tools. By using specific, practiced skills, individuals learn from Moore the EQ skills needed to inspire, engage, relate, and ultimately increase productivity and profitability.

To schedule Roberta Moore for a speaking engagement, please email bgrunzinger@arcoandassociates.com or call 636-527-9254 x3.

rmoore@eqicoach.com
www.eqicoach.com/

www.linkedin.com/in/robertamoore/
www.linkedin.com/company/the-eq-i-coach/
www.facebook.com/roberta.moore.1272
www.facebook.com/consciouschoicesstl/
www.facebook.com/groups/540133839706561/

Black Girl in Techlandia

I never intended or dreamed of being an entrepreneur nor owning a technology company. I have accomplished this distinct honor, though, and I now help others who desire to become entrepreneurs as well. My journey has been adventurous and reflects all the life lessons garnered from family, friends, mentors, and the hard knocks along the way. The core of it all emanates from my love of technology and science fiction. *Star Trek* was a game-changer for me and so began the journey of being a life-long tech junkie.

In 2002, I was encouraged to start my own company. My boss at that time said, "It's time you start your own business—you are just like I was when I started mine." He then helped me start the company and became my first customer. Abaxent LLC (my company) has been operating for nearly eighteen years. Although I am the owner, my title is "Chief Problem-Solver." My curiosity and zeal to help people solve problems has been a guiding tenet of my business.

Becoming an entrepreneur in the technology sector was beyond what I could have imagined for myself. Being Black and raised by a single Black teenage mom in the1950s were not considered to be the building blocks of success. How does one beat those odds? My family was headed by a strong matriarch: my grandmother. She was one of thirteen children. At the age of fourteen, my grandmother migrated from Canada to St. Louis with her sister. My grandmother was fearless—and an original self-sufficient business entrepreneur. She owned three businesses: a domestic-service business, a hairdressing business, and a catering business. She also raised me and took me with her everywhere she could. My grandmother was my first role model of a savvy and independent entrepreneur. Given her diverse clientele, I was exposed to several ethnic and religious cultures.

Having a young mother helped me to learn the importance of social skills and networks. My mother, more of a big sister, gave birth to me when she was sixteen. Her inner circle of friends was pivotal in my life. They rallied around my mom and became my extended "aunts and uncles." We all grew up together. Within African-American culture, blood lines did not determine familial relationships. My mother's friends loved and invested in me throughout my entire life. They contributed to my development by teaching me social skills and necessary abilities to navigate the world around me. It is from these aunts and uncles that I learned two key lessons: Do the right thing and take care of anyone in need. They modeled these lessons without fail. The nature of my community was not based on how much money you could make, but the importance of love, loyalty, and support. This sense of caring for one another and an obligation to serve the community were essential for survival. To this day, these aunts and uncles are still part of my life.

I grew up in St. Louis during the 1950s and 1960s of the Civil Rights Movement. This period of St. Louis history was turbulent and dangerous for African-Americans. The need to possess skills for independence, self-sufficiency, social skills, and a sense of collective well-being were just as important as the emerging technical skills I sought. Although the fight for Civil Rights loomed large in St. Louis, I found solace in my curiosity about the world around me. I would often wonder how things fit together and the future possibilities. I was a voracious reader and obsessed over sci-fi-related literature about the Universe, interstellar travel, technological machines, and alien cultures. I loved Isaac Asimov's *I, Robot* and *The Foundation Trilogy* (the basics of computers before computer reality).

I also loved hands-on projects that involved auto mechanics, appliances, and science experiments. In high school, I was forced to sign up for home economics. Instead, I wanted to join my guy friends in auto shop. Girls did not take auto shop. When I expressed my dismay to my grandmother, she mentioned it to her boss, a lawyer. He paid a visit to my school and what do you know—I was the first girl let into shop! Having adults support the idea of girls having a choice and the notion that I can try all things helped to secure my mind-set of not having to acquiesce to social norms regarding gender. It's important to have the space to dream.

My passion for science-fiction reading and vocational training soared to new heights when something unexpected caught my attention: I discovered a television program in the late sixties called *Star Trek*, which was life-changing for me. I saw a command bridge on a starship that had multiple races, genders and even an alien!! Lieutenant Uhura!! Wow, a Black female in command of communications on the most awesome ship in the galaxy! Who knew we could do that? I saw, I believed, and I dared to dream. This can be me! Just last year, I fulfilled a life dream to let Nichelle Nichols— Lieutenant Uhura—know that I became an engineer because of her portrayal of this very important character in this Universe. Representation matters.

I loved the message of hope in the future that sci-fi portrayed: We can all get along and live together; women are just as capable as men; aliens can be cool; and being different is okay. How cool!

Education is the way into technology!

I was college-bound after having earned a merit-based scholarship. As part of college prep, I attended a one-week STEM summer camp showcasing multiple engineering disciplines. Computers caught my attention. I learned to "talk" directly to the computer hardware and found my calling.

Choosing Missouri University of Science and Technology—formerly University of Missouri-Rolla—was an eye-opening experience. There was one other Black female on campus at the time and she was a senior. Our freshman class recorded one of the largest women-to-men ratios in the university's history; that is, one female to ten males. One of the keys to my college success was a Black couple who lived off campus that oversaw the only Black fraternity house at the university. They were always supportive and available. I never hesitated to interact with them as much as possible. The pair became like family to all the Black students. I emulated how they were successful in such an environment.

During those college days, I developed several great male mentors that were helpful and provided guidance, acclimating me to campus life. I learned to blend in when possible, stand my ground when needed, and find my voice as required.

My academic success at college began to speak for itself. I gained the support of my first long-time advisor. As a member of several design groups where we all shared a strong common interest in science fiction and discussions about the future. I survived and grew in this environment.

While in college, I found my life partner, my soul mate, and my match. He liked that I was intelligent, independent, and that I had my own ideas about the world. l learned a new way to collaborate and work as a team. Except now, my husband and I were the team.

Being in a science and technology field, I was around men. My husband was an engineer and helped me to better understand men from a workplace standpoint and how to navigate a male-centric environment. He provided insight into the male "playbook." This education came in handy throughout my career.

My job at General Electric (GE) Healthcare, working with medical imaging equipment and obtaining a patent, led me to seek a graduate degree from Marquette University. I applied and was accepted into the new Biomedical Engineering program. I was fascinated by the connection between technology and biology. The combination of work and school was fun and exciting. Again, I was one of few women at work and the only minority female engineer. Most of the women at GE during that time period were secretaries—and I was happy to be around any women at all. Once again, I made history: Not only was I a member of the initial graduating class of the Biomedical Engineering program, but I was the only minority female in that class as well.

Of all the roles I had at GE, I had the opportunity to find one of my niche callings, which is a translation of very technical things into common speak. It was the first time I had created a job for myself. I became the liaison between the sales team and the engineers. I loved this role!! From that point on, I created all my roles because I saw a need, as opposed to having a job that somebody else held with somebody else's expectations.

I spent about a decade with GE Healthcare and had the opportunity to work with super smart guys. During an off-site discussion (being engineers, even off work we discussed work), we brainstormed to create a cheaper way to run systems. We came up with an idea that led to a patent for us!! To this day, the Magnetic Resonance Suite Lighting system is in use.

I had an exceptional career at GE; however, I wanted more adventures.

In 1985, A.O. Smith hired me, when I was six months pregnant with my second child, to manage PhDs and college students who were working on the first supercomputer. My team participated in the creation of, among many things, what was to become the ATM banking system.

My technology journey next lead me to IBM. What drew me there? Well, at IBM I got the chance to work directly with computers. I had an exceptional mentor that had experience working at a different IBM location. He was strong in finance and process. We became fast friends; and with his guidance, I was able to move into new roles that I created, based on my insights of understanding both the customer and our processes. My skill as technology process interpreter was well received and recognized. I could assess technical problems, create a process, and design a solution that was understandable.

On the home front, as I became more involved with my growing kids, I wanted more flexibility. I researched a local college, Alverno College, a 130-plus-year-old women's college, to explore a teaching certificate to teach STEM at a high school. Timing always being everything, when Alverno College learned of my technical background, I was enlisted to assist with their in-house technology issues, which lead to teaching at the college level for the next twenty-three years! I started working at Alverno College in 1993; I retired in 2016 as Professor Emeritus. I had been the first engineer they hired. Under my leadership, I developed the technology curriculum for several degree majors and minors, along with a hands-on learning lab.

Although throughout my career there I worked to establish a technology department, I gained much more from working at the women's college. It was a wonderful and unexpected experience. I had no idea how much I would love training and working with all women. I became a teacher and mentor for women of all ages. I had the opportunity to teach my love of technology, to have other women fall in love with the discipline, and to demonstrate that this was not just a man's field. I am very proud of the young women that allowed me to help them grow and shape the realm of modern technology.

My twenty-three years at Alverno paralleled my work at IBM and brought about moves to several smaller companies thereafter, which prepared me to take on several executive roles. It is from these experiences I found that true sales allow you to solve problems. I love to solve problems!

I learned to love the challenge of not being what others expect and to become the change that is needed. I also learned to not be afraid of uncharted territory because the road is always different, exciting above all else, and new—like the unexplored Universe the *Star Trek* crew might discover.

As a lifelong Trekkie, the words from the 1966 television series spoke to me on many levels, "To go boldly where no man has gone before."

Technology and science fiction have been the impetus for me to explore possibilities and not be limited to current norms. I am a HUGE *Star Trek* fan. I have boldly gone where few have gone before. I am a trailblazer. Nothing is impossible!

My life now reflects what Jean-Luc Picard, Captain Federation Starfleet USS Enterprise spoke: "Things are only impossible until they're not."

Adonica Randall is President and Chief Problem Solver of Abaxent, LLC, an 18-year-old certified MBE/WBE technology solutions company. With over 35 years of technical and business experience she has specialized in development of business startups, new services and process improvement, with experience across a variety of industries including healthcare, insurance, manufacturing and construction.

Adonica has served in technical, sales and management positions at General Motors, GE Medical Systems, IBM and the AO Smith Engineering Division as well as starting multiple Professional Services businesses.

Adonica received her Master of Engineering degree in Biomedical Engineering from Marquette University and her B.S. in Computer Science from Missouri School of Science and Technology. Adonica is a Professor Emeritus from Alverno College Business School – Computing and Information Technology and Business Analytics.

Notable service: Entrepreneur in Residence at Marquette University, Minority Business Economic Input Committee 2nd Vice Chair for North Central Minority Supplier Development Council, and Ambassador for Women's Business Enterprise National Council (Wisconsin) and local community organizations.

She is a well-recognized as a thought leader that speaks widely on the future of women in STEM careers.

Adonica has been married for 44 years, has launched two adult children, and has two granddaughters destined for STEM!

arandall@abaxent.com

www.abaxent-global.com

www.linkedin.com/in/adonicarandall

Heart of an Entrepreneur

How do we remain relevant in a rapidly changing industry? What are the secrets to remaining flexible and successful while riding the waves of change? Change has crashed in tsunami-like waves through my journey as an entrepreneur, and I would like to share some of what I've learned.

The truth is that I've had the heart of an entrepreneur for almost as long as I can remember. It was the early 1980s, and I was in third grade when I came across an incentive program for kids involving selling gift wrap and greeting cards. The plan was simple: Sell to your friends and family, then choose an incentive gift from a catalogue.

There were just two problems: 1) I was tremendously shy, and 2) I did not have a lot of easy targets in need of gift wrap or greeting cards. Nonetheless, I'd spotted a must-have red microscope in the incentive gift catalogue.

Conjuring up every bit of my courage, I walked down McKinley Street going door-to-door in search of willing buyers. There were times when I stood on a porch for several minutes with my knees quite literally knocking while willing myself to ring the doorbell. Whether through pity or my impressive nine-year old sales skills, I sold enough gift wrap and greeting cards to earn that red microscope, and I was on cloud nine!

In high school, a friend and I saw a need for more snacks than the single vending machine in our small school could provide. We developed a plan to sell chips, sweet treats, and ramen noodles. We ran our snack shop before school, during lunch, and after school out of a spare locker.

When I landed my first real job out of college, I dreamed of somehow working for myself. I had no idea what that might look like, but I knew this was ultimately part of the path I would find. As is often the case, opportunity for me arrived in disguise, appearing ever-so-much like interruption, dashed hopes, and sometimes even failure.

I dipped my toes in the consulting space when I quit my job to become a stay-at-home mom in 2001. My boss had asked me to consider working on a contracted basis. Long before telecommuting was a thing, I began to telecommute as an independent contractor.

A few years later, I was invited to come back as a full-time employee. Temporarily forgetting about my dream to be a business owner and lured by promises of certainty, benefits, and someone else contributing to my 401(k), I agreed. About a year later, I learned one of the dirty little secrets of business: *the sure thing isn't all that sure.* One morning, I was advised that the company was filing bankruptcy and my position was being eliminated. I placed a few calls to colleagues in the telecommunications industry letting them know that I was available for consulting work.

By noon that day, I had lined up a year-long consulting gig with a telecommunications company. I would be handling the same product development, contract negotiation, and marketing responsibilities that had been part of my just-eliminated position. I received a call later that same day from the employer who had fired me that morning. They admitted that they hadn't realized all of the work I had handled and wished to rescind their decision to eliminate my position. In one of the more delicious moments of my business career, I told them that I'd already secured a new position and that I would be moving on to my new consulting role. They signed on as my second client. Those two clients soon turned into five clients. With that, I had found the path I'd been looking for since leaving my locker-based snack shop venture.

With these initial successes, business was booming, and I had no plans to make any changes when I received a call from a start-up telecommunications company, based twenty minutes from my back door, inviting me to join them. I thanked them, said how honored I was that they would think of me and gently turned down the opportunity. I was happy with my little stable of clients and had no interest in abandoning them. A few months later, the same start-up group came back to me and begged me to reconsider. Again lured by their ambitious five-year plan and an offer I couldn't refuse, I fired all my clients and joined them.

Within six months, we were advised that the company would be sold by year-end and that we should all update our resumes. Remember the lesson that I said I'd learned previously? *The sure thing is not always the sure thing.* Here I was, learning this lesson again. This time, I decided that there was no going back. I wasn't going to be held hostage by job moves, bankruptcies, or fast-forwarding five-year plans. I knew the need for my services was out there. I knew I could make a good living. I knew that this is what my heart called for behind each of the (not-so) sure things.

Ladies and gentlemen, the girl with the gift wrap catalogs and snack-filled locker was BACK! And, if I'm honest, my knees were still knocking from time to time.

Joining forces with a fellow colleague, also displaced, we formed Leverage Cable Consulting in the summer of 2011 and have never looked back.

In our industry, it is not uncommon for people to take the approach I did—a little consulting here, a little traditional office work there. There's no harm in this, but it isn't being a business owner. Today, I regularly tell clients that running my consulting firm is not my job in between jobs—it IS my job. When I had put the business-owner hat on this time, it was for good.

It turns out that, even as a business owner, the sure thing is not always the sure thing. It's true in business, as in life, that we are all in a constant state of evolution. If there is a constant, the constant is change. Change will impact your business and must be embraced.

I started in the cable and telecommunications industry when most cable television subscribers had sixty to seventy channels and when Netflix was a subscription of DVDs received in the mail each month. There were no smartphones or iPads.

The telecommunications industry has been through some intense change over the nearly twenty-two years that I've been a part of this industry. We've gone from sixty or so channels to hundreds of channels. High-definition (HD) content is ubiquitous. Internet service has transformed from dial-up to "always on" high-speed Internet. Most of us travel with a small screen in the form of our smartphones. All of these changes pale in comparison to the changes that we've seen over the last two years and that continue to present day. Today, my industry is in the midst of a seismic shift as television content, consumed on the couch in the living room, becomes streaming content that we can watch on our phones, on our laptops or iPads. Netflix is available with the click of a button, as are hundreds of other television-viewing apps.

What's stayed constant? Change. Change is the constant.

You may not be a part of the ever-changing telecommunications industry, but you will face change. How do we continue to do great work and maintain a steadiness even as the ground moves beneath us? I'm confident that, even as change continues, my secrets to remaining relevant and agile are timeless tactics that are universally true. What are some essentials to business success? What are those mindsets and approaches that always will be in demand?

Four Timeless Tactics

1. Be a problem-solver.

I do not think of myself as a salesperson. In fact, when I lapse into sales mode, it is not a good look and it is not a role in which I feel comfortable. I LOVE to solve problems! I am perfectly comfortable serving as a problem-solver. Whether it is business-to-business service offerings or a widget to make life easier for the general public, business success often comes from solving problems. Who doesn't want an easy button? As an entrepreneur, success in identifying the problem comes from listening. When I approach a potential client from a posture of listening, I can more easily identify how their needs may intersect with my ability to problem-solve. From there, the sale may close itself.

2. Be a learner.

Read. Listen. Ask questions. In his book, *Good to Great: Why Some Companies Make the Leap…and Others Don't*, Jim Collins says, "I don't know where we should take this company, but I do know that if I start with the right people, ask them the right questions, and engage them in vigorous debate, we will find a way to make the company great."

I want to be a life-long learner rather than being someone who always knows the answer. Although my clients look to me for expertise and answers, I am misguided if I fail to welcome what they may teach me.

3. Be dependable.

On a recent business trip, I stayed in a Marriott-owned hotel. On their wall was a quote from J. Willard Marriott: "It's the little things that make the big things possible." I am not perfectly dependable, but it is my goal. Dependability builds trust among clients and future clients. This has been particularly important for me because, most days, I work from my home office. Despite any urban legends that you may have heard, most people working from a home office are not kicking back on the couch in their pajamas. I want to be known as someone who is on top of things. I want clients to be shocked that I am able to crank out the work I do, rather than feeling that I do "okay" for someone who works from home. Trust is built over time with many little things done correctly. Dependability and the trust that it builds is essential to remaining relevant to the needs of clients or customers.

3. Recognize and promote the unique gifts you bring to the table.

I have often been guilty of assuming that anyone could do what, I do if only they put their mind to it. I tend to believe that "everyone knows" the things I know, and I can quickly forget the value I bring to a client relationship. In *Dare to Lead: Brave Work. Tough Conversations. Whole Hearts*, Brené Brown echoed this idea, "Remember too that sometimes we overlook our own strengths because we take them for granted and forget that they're special." If everyone were able to do it, they would. As change occurs, the unique gifts each of us brings may have new applications. Find those special strengths that are unique to your skill set. Chances are, those skills will transition and morph along with the changes that come.

A few years ago, I hired a consultant to assist me with a particularly busy season. Like me, he had spent most of his career in telecommunications. When change swept through his company and his position was eliminated, he struggled to see what was next. I was grateful for his familiar skills to assist me through this busy period. A few months after his project with me wrapped up, I heard from him again. He had landed a new position with a nationally known insurance company—completely outside the telecommunications industry. He was asked to roll out a new product and was amazed at how the skill set he saw as highly specific to telecommunications translated directly into a skill set needed in a completely different industry. He managed to recognize and promote those unique gifts that made him successful in cable television, and he re-deployed them in a new arena.

Your strengths are uniquely yours. Don't discount them. Those are the ingredients to success in a changing world.

★★★★★

I long for a crystal ball. To peer into the future. To see what is next. I would be most comfortable with my world staying the same, but our world is rapidly changing. This year's latest cell phone is next year's outdated technology. Remaining relevant means remaining flexible. "Flexible" does not mean our journeys are dictated by outside forces. It means that we must focus on timeless ingredients to success: solving problems, remaining a lifelong learner, creating a reputation for dependability, and focusing on our unique strengths. They were unlikely suspects, but a red microscope and locker-based snack business turned out to be exactly what I needed on my path to creating the heart of an entrepreneur.

 Cheryl Summers is principal and partner at Leverage Cable Consulting and chief executive officer at Leverage Broadband Strategies. Cheryl traces her entrepreneurial spirit back to her childhood days of selling gift wrap to her neighbors. Today, her expertise lies in telecommunications operations, management or ownership transitions, and contract negotiation. She has been in the trenches of the telecommunications industry since 1998, and formed Leverage in 2011.

Before establishing Leverage Cable Consulting, Cheryl served as Vice President of Programming for Cobridge Communications and Director of Programming for Broadstripe, both St. Louis-based cable and internet providers.

Cheryl serves on the board of directors for Christians in Communication and is active in the Mid-America Cable Telecommunications Association. When she is not solving problems in the telecommunications industry, she is an outspoken advocate for those who have experienced abuse. In 2018, she founded *For Such a Time As This Rally*, a group working to eradicate abuse in church settings. Cheryl has spent the last 10 years leading divorce recovery support groups and currently leads a group at First Free Church where she is an active member. She lives in Ballwin, MO with her husband, two teenage daughters, and two overindulged cats.

cherylsummers@leveragecableconsulting.com
www.leveragecableconsulting.com

Continued on next page

www.linkedin.com/in/cherylsummers
www.linkedin.com/company/leverage-cable-consulting
www.facebook.com/cheryl.b.summers

The Divine Feminine Energy of Finance

"I've been trying to buy a house for the past eighteen months, and I'm not having any luck! I've been going through the process, doing everything, yet nothing seems to be working. I'm spinning my wheels! All the pieces of the puzzle are here, yet I still don't have my home!"

It was my first time speaking with Ms. G, but it wasn't the first time hearing this cry for help. Working in financial services for the past seventeen years, I knew exactly what Ms. G's issue was. It had nothing to do with her credit score or income—she wasn't operating in the right energy.

Ms. G wanted to buy a house, but she had blockages. I know she had blockages because, well, if she didn't have any blockages, then she would've been enjoying her new house. You see, no matter how great her realtor was or how high her credit score peaked, and regardless of her six-figure salary, she wasn't ready to purchase her first house, well, because she wasn't ready. Her inner-being wasn't aligned with her desired outcome (homebuying). And no matter how hard we try, if there is misalignment, we'll never achieve the result we truly desire and deserve. It's like attempting to listen to country western music on the classical radio station. We can hope, wish, and commit to calling the classical radio station day after day to request our favorite country western song, but guess what? We'll still find ourselves listening to Beethoven. In order to achieve the desired result, our inner-being must be aligned to the vibrational frequency of our desired (outer) result.

Aligning her inner and outer worlds would require Ms. G to step away from making and forcing things to happen and, instead, to embody the energy of creation. She would need to release the competitive masculine energy that society pushes and tap into her divine feminine energy of creating.

Masculine and feminine energies aren't about gender. These energies are possessed by everyone regardless of gender. Think of masculine (structured, logical, and competitive) and feminine (flowy, feeling-based, and creative) energies as the yin-yang symbol. Although most people view the yin-yang symbol as a balance of good and bad (in every good there's a bad and in every bad there's a good), the essence of the symbol is to visually (humans like visuals) express the necessity of the interrelationship of masculine and feminine for balance.

We've been taught that money is a man's game. From the boardroom to the media, the world never misses an opportunity to program thoughts into our subconscious minds that tell us that money is a man's game, played by men in dark suits—and if women dare attempt to step foot out of the house and do something else besides being a homemaker, men would reluctantly let us in and then pay us less while hoping nobody notices.

Over time, the essence of money and financial planning has adopted a masculine dominant energy. The issue with this is, in our ever-changing reality, continuous creation is key. Financial planning is a creative, flowing process of divine feminine energy. Feminine energy is creative energy. Creation starts with self; and before we can create anything, we must first go within.

Masculine energy looks outside; it rushes, and it competes with external factors.

Feminine energy doesn't compete; it is introspective. It evaluates, calls in, and creates. Using feminine energy when planning will ignite massive success in our lives.

After eighteen months of spinning her wheels, I successfully worked with Ms. G to achieve her goal of homeownership. We accomplished this within twelve weeks.

If you're seeking change in any area of your life, I urge you to not only continue reading this book, but also to take inspired action to change your life.

From birth, we're exposed to different beliefs and patterns regarding money and finances. Most of these beliefs aren't ours—they're the (limiting) beliefs of others that we've adopted along the way because, frankly, we didn't know any better. If we want to have financial success and redefine the American Dream on our terms, the first thing we'll need to do is identify and become aware of what's standing in between us and abundance.

Were you taught things like "money doesn't grow on trees?" Or were you told that your family couldn't "afford" certain things? Perhaps you were made to believe that a certain level of wealth was reserved for a select class or group of people. Old sayings and beliefs are standing in the way of your abundance birthright. To change your destiny, you must uncover these beliefs before activating your abundance.

During our first session, Ms. G and I uncovered her deep-rooted beliefs about money. She was going through the motions of homebuying; yet internally, she felt as though the process was difficult. Despite being gainfully employed and meeting the credit and cash qualifications for homeownership, she felt that she had a one-in-a-million chance of owning a home. She'd heard (and believed) horror stories. Interestingly, these beliefs were all based on others' experiences. She said things like "I know it's not an easy process; it takes a lot of work and finding a reasonably priced property that suits me in Miami is like finding a needle in a haystack." She believed that despite her financial readiness, her mortgage application would be frowned upon because she was unmarried. I reminded her that not long ago, just three decades ago, the Women's Business Ownership Act of 1988 (HR 5050) was passed to eliminate the need for women to have male co-signers.

Ms. G, the director and star of the show, didn't truly believe that she had a chance at homeownership; therefore, everything was happening as she was directing it. No wonder she'd been on a merry-go-round for the past eighteen months!

What limiting beliefs are holding you back? I'll give you some examples; however, you'll need to sit down and think about the limiting beliefs that exist in *your* world. An ideal way to do this would be to keep a money journal for seven days. Within this money journal, you are going to write down everything you think, say, or feel whenever money comes up. This includes conversations with others, as well as with yourself. Are you saying things like "I can't afford that" when your children ask for things? How do you feel when it's time to pay your monthly bills? Do you pay them with a willing heart and a smile on your face or are you full of grudge and anger? Write it all down.

I gave Ms. G this homework. I asked her to rewrite her "Money Story." I encourage you to do the same.

After uncovering the limiting beliefs that we've been carrying, it's time to create a new story. As we move from stories that are keeping us out of alignment with our desired outcome, we're going to reprogram our subconscious mind by creating new beliefs.

To do this, I'd like you to imagine yourself two years into the future. We are both enjoying the vacation of a lifetime, and we bump into each other. You eagerly start filling me in about your professional and personal life. Write as if you're playing catch-up with a long-lost friend. How does that look to you? You're on vacation so you have plenty of time.

Imagining yourself in the destination of your dreams is a powerful visualization tool. Visualization is essential to living the life you deserve. Many believe that you must "see it to believe it," when the secret truth is "you must believe it to see it." Visualize yourself at your desired destination and get ready!

It's time to rewrite your Money Story. Has it occurred to you that you're the only person, force, or influence keeping you from your abundance? Think about it. If you wanted to get up right now and move across the room, you could, couldn't you? Let's say you're in a wheelchair. Would that stop you from moving across the room? Sure, you may not be able to walk across the room, but you could wheel across the room. What if you're bedridden? You may not be able to walk or wheel across the room, but you could use your resources to reposition your bed so that you're on the other side of the room, correct? The point is: If you really felt that you deserved to be on the other side of the room, you'd make it happen.

People struggle with their financial goals because they don't believe that they're worthy of financial freedom. The struggle with worthiness is keeping them from abundance.

Decide you're worthy of abundance. You must step into your worthiness! Your worthiness will unlock the door to your riches. Assess if you're living in your worthiness or suffering from what my friend and author Michelle Hollinger calls "wounded worthiness" by looking at your current income. If you're a W-2 wage earner, pull out your paycheck stubs; if you're self-employed, pull out your most recent bank or merchant processing (PayPal, etc.) statement.

Today, money moves electronically. We rarely see it and most people think about money in terms of scarcity: "Will I have enough to pay my rent this month?" Folks fall into the rhythm of receiving direct deposits and transfers, then immediately spending funds instead of taking time to review, evaluate, and connect to the numbers. Numbers don't lie; in fact, they tell a noteworthy story. We are paid based on the value we provide or the pay that we deem ourselves worthy of receiving.

If you review your numbers and feel shortchanged, then ask yourself a very important question: *Why am I allowing myself to be underpaid?*

The question is about you and the reasons you've allowed yourself to be undervalued. It's not about your employer or your clients. Perhaps you're allowing yourself to be underpaid because you've grown stagnant and stopped adding value *to yourself* which limits the value that you offer—and are paid for. Maybe you believe that your clients won't pay your increased price.

Grab your favorite journal, notebook, napkin, or sheet of paper and write down your response to why you allow yourself to be underpaid. Ponder the question in real time, with raw emotions and answers. After you've written your response, commit to reading it daily for one week. You must sit with your truth.

Tip: When pricing your services as an entrepreneur, don't allow fear that the client won't pay your price to dictate your fee. If you're committed to consistently providing value, then raise your prices to a fee that correlates to the value you provide. When you do this, the only people you'll lose are those who didn't value your work. Their departure will make room for you to attract people who understand your value and will happily pay you. You'll end up with less people while making more money. Magic!

Evaluating and making changes to your current income is an important foundational step in activating your worthiness. It empowers you to ask for—and receive—what you're worthy of. You'll build momentum and begin asking for all kinds of things you're worthy of receiving.

Now you're ready to **maintain the vibration of abundance.** To activate abundance in all areas of your life, you'll have to control your mind. Your mind-set determines the life that you live. Whatever your current position in life, one thing is for certain: It all started in your mind. Your life is a direct reflection of the thoughts and stories you tell yourself and believe. Think about how you were dealing with money before reading this chapter. Were you operating from a scarcity mind-set by playing defense with your thoughts and actions? Did you spend your time and energy thinking about money that you don't have instead of planning for the money you desire?

The number one difference between the poor, the middle class, and the wealthy is mind-set. Every journey starts in the mind. Before you jump into stocks, bonds, and other financial tools, you must first get your mind right!

Are you committed to tapping into your divine feminine energy? Unlimited abundance awaits!

Hyacinth has assisted thousands of professionals and entrepreneurs jump off the hamster wheel of lack and free themselves from economic bondage by making a lasting Shift to Abundance™. She and her team of professionals at The Henderson Financial Group understand that the real key to financial freedom is achieved, not by working *hard* for your money, but by <u>making your money work for you</u>!

Hyacinth, takes her clients on a journey of uncovering, releasing and reprogramming limiting beliefs so they can experience a complete mind-set shift and take control of their financial future once and for all. She also places a strong emphasis on the importance of radical student loan & credit card debt elimination.

Hyacinth is a licensed Stockbroker, a Registered Investment Adviser and a licensed Life, Health & Annuity Broker with over seventeen years of experience in the industry.

It takes **CREAM** to create your ideal version of The American Dream and Hyacinth takes you on a journey of enlightenment and education on her popular financial education radio show and podcast The American CREAM: **C**redit, **R**eal estate, **E**ntrepreneurship, **A**ssets and **M**indset.

Hyacinth is a daughter, mother, leader, spiritual hippie, enthusiast, life-long learner and book hoarder, lover of food, sun, salt and the unknown, and an extroverted introvert.

HH@HyacinthHenderson.com
www.HyacinthHenderson.com
www.TheHendersonFinancialGroup.com

Continued on next page

www.facebook.com/HyacinthLikeTheFlower
www.linkedin.com/in/hyacinth-henderson/
www.instagram.com/Hyacinth.Henderson
www.Youtube.com/HyacinthHenderson

Loving Failure

In my life, I learned that failure was not acceptable. My family was very competitive. We loved to play games, not baseball or football, but cards and board games. We played to win. In fact, when my husband met my family for the first time, he said he had never met a family that played full contact Scrabble. Like I said, we liked to win. No one made it life or death, but we were competitive.

Major life decisions were made based on how successful I thought I would be. In college, I didn't pick marketing as a major because there was a chance I could be fired in my career. Obviously, I had never heard of downsizing. My major became accounting. It involved numbers, which I loved, and there was a demand for good accountants. A very practical and safe career for thirty years.

In 2016, a made a crazy decision to give up my safe W-2 career and start a journey that would teach me how to embrace failure. You see, I had decided to start my own business and subsequently became a partner at B2B CFO. I would be responsible for finding my own clients, marketing, branding, and selling. There was not a safety net or paycheck. Without clients, I would not be making a living.

It would be a crash course on learning how to be a successful entrepreneur. This was a road that I had never travelled. It would be fraught with disappointments, unsuccessful meetings, and failed proposals. My family was counting on me to make this work. Failure was not an option. I was about to learn the most valuable lessons of my life. If I wasn't failing, I wasn't taking risks. If I wasn't willing to get out of my comfort zone and go meet strangers, set up meetings, and follow-up with people, I would not be successful.

Our brains are programmed to protect us. How do they do that? They have us scroll through a litany of reasons that prevent us from trying something new. What will the other person think? There is no way that will work. What if I fail? There are so many things that could go wrong. Our head will fill us with so much trash sometimes, that if we listen to it, we will never be successful.

Most of us have a bad connotation with the word failure. We act like it is a scarlet letter, rather than a badge of courage. It takes a lot of courage to fail. Risks allow us to live more fulfilled lives and not wonder what might have been. I recently heard a survey of people that had just turned 80. When asked what they most regretted in life, the answer was the same. They regretted not taking some of the risks that they faced in their life, because now they will never know the outcome.

Looking back now that first 10 months was full of failures. When I had my first meetings, I was unpolished, unsure of myself, and quite frankly didn't understand how the process we were taught to use to facilitate a successful meeting would work. I remember a meeting with a person that I truly respected from a previous employer. After we talked and I presented my explanation of my services, he looked at me and said that I would never be able to sell anything. My presentation was terrible. I was devastated.

He made a great point. I failed to explain how I help business owners; I had not actively listened to him, I was busy talking about my new business and myself. That failure, made me re-examine my presentation, practice more and be prepared. His honestly, helped me improve. I failed, but I knew my next steps to be successful in the next meeting.

That is what failure is all about. Truly successful people fail as often as they are successful. One of the most successful women I know, Maxine Clark, Chairman of the Board of Build a Bear, made her own success. When she was initially starting Build a Bear, she was told her idea of making your own bear would never be successful. She could not get financing for her new venture. She withdrew money from her own retirement account to start the business that would later become a worldwide phenomenon.

One of my struggles with my business was my sales closing rate. That rate determined if I would have clients to work with and make money. My closing rate the first year of my business was zero percent. My closing rate my second and third year was less than 50%. This was well below successful partners in our firm. I was failing because I wasn't listening to the business owner and finding their need. This failure taught me that it didn't matter what I thought the need was for a business owner. What mattered was the need the business owner wanted to solve. Honing my listening skills by truly paying attention to the owners needs I was able to design tailored solutions, just for them. My closing rate this year is 89%.

Failure is not about being right or wrong. It is about taking action and doing things that make you uncomfortable. When you move out of your comfort zone you are taking risks. When you take risks, you move your life and business forward.

Recently I took a marketing class. It was a 30 day challenge and it covered websites, social media, networking, and making videos. All of this was out of my comfort zone. Marketing was like learning a foreign language.

I decided that I would create a video. I had never recorded myself before. I upgraded my phone to the new iPhone 11 Pro, bought a light, a tripod and a microphone. That equipment looked so sexy when it arrived. Then it came time to do the video.

To put this in context, I am not crazy about having my picture taken, let alone seeing myself on video. I put on a suit, practiced about 5 times and plunged in. Satisfied with my first try, I sent the video off to be reviewed by my marketing coach and my marketing department.

That night I showed my son. He was appalled. He said "Mom stop reading a script. You need to look at the camera. You really didn't send this to any one did you?" After relooking at it, I started laughing. I mean that deep down belly laugh that had my whole body shaking. Actually, I couldn't stop laughing for several minutes.

The video was truly awful. I looked like I had 2 black eyes and I was not looking at the camera. The best part of all the feedback? I was not reading a script. I was so terrified by the experience of recording myself; I was stiff and rigid in the video. Everyone assumed I was reading a script.

The next day I called Misty Kortes, from Your Marketing Coach, www.yourmarketingcoachonline.com, and our marketing department at B2B CFO. Truly feeling sorry for them and laughing at myself. I don't know how they would have provided constructive criticism. That day, after many more takes and laughing at myself some more, I produced a much better product. According to Misty it was 10,000% better.

If I hadn't failed so spectacularly the first time, I wouldn't have been able to relax and do a successful video. If I had let my fear get the best of me, I wouldn't have even started. I plan to hone this new skill and use video to connect with people.

The second thing this class challenged me to do was to leverage my current network. During the class, I received an email from the "St Louis Small Business Monthly", a local monthly newspaper in St. Louis. They were looking for the Top 20 Business Advisors in St Louis. I did something that I had refused to do before. I reached out to my clients and friends and asked them to nominate me if they thought I deserved it. In addition, I asked them if there was anything that I could do to help them. In late November, I received notification that I would be honored as one of the Top 20 Business Advisors in St Louis, in the February 2020 "St Louis Small Business Monthly". It is an incredible honor to be recognized. Because I chose to act and ignore the reasons that my brain told me I would not qualify, I received this great opportunity.

Recently, I was challenged to come up with an acronym for failure. Here's my new motto:

F – Future

A – Accomplishments

I – Include

L – Lots of

U – Unsuccessful

R – Roads to

E – Explore

This past year, I have been working on a book about successful women. The theory of the book is that anyone can have a successful life. You do not have to have a six figure income, a fancy title, or be the head of a successful company to live a successful life. You determine what your successful life looks like.

I interviewed women and talked about their road to success. One of the questions I asked was, "Are you willing to share a failure that has propelled you to success?" None of the women interviewed were willing to share a true failure story. I failed in the way I crafted my question, or they weren't willing to be that vulnerable. This failure inspired me to change directions and concentrate instead on failure.

Embracing failure is the key to any success. When we fail, we change direction and pick a new road. All the women I interviewed overcame many obstacles to be successful in their lives. One interesting fact was that they didn't talk about obstacles, they talked about their accomplishments. They were focused on being successful. Although, they had amazing stories, I want to share that none of them was an overnight success. They had worked hard and grabbed opportunities along the way. Sometimes they changed total directions in their careers.

The stories about their failures would have more impact and importance to women. Many of them shared that they where fortunate and that they were in the right place at the right time. I would also argue that luck had nothing to do with their success. They worked hard and made themselves known to the world. Then the world noticed and gave them the outcome they desired. Success did not come to them overnight. Their life journeys like our own were filled with disappointments, failures, and fear of taking risks. Their persistence and unwillingness to let fear prevent them from moving forward is the driver of their success.

Think of what you could accomplish if you stopped letting the fear of failure drive your decisions. What's the worst that could happen? You might fail, but more importantly you will know the outcome.

Failure is your life journey to living a successful life. People that are having their 80th birthdays know the secret. Not taking risk is the true road to failure. You will never know what you could have accomplished. Live your life now with no regrets. Fail often, fail forward and you will succeed beyond your wildest expectations. And for goodness sake, don't forget to laugh at yourself. Failure truly is the best comic relief.

 Debi Corrie is a business owner and partner at B2B CFO® with more than 30 years of finance experience. Debi is a strategist, board member, and public speaker. She owns 2 other businesses Taxpertise, LLP and DJC Media, LLC. She is dedicated to helping others learn how to create their own brand of success through strategy, education, coaching, and writing. She is the recipient of the 2019 Impact St Louis – Person of Inspiration Award and recognized by the *St. Louis Small Business Monthly* as a Top St. Louis Business Advisor for 2020. A lifelong learner, Debi believes that everyone can create a successful life.

debi@debicorrie.com
www.debicorrie.com

www.facebook.com/DebiCorrie1/
www.instagram.com/debicorrie/
www.twitter.com/DebiCorrie
www.linkedin.com/in/debicorriecfo/

Lisa Frumhoff

Real Connections Matter

I found two keys to business that changed everything: first, real connections matter more than a business-friendly front and secondly, when you follow your true passion you create authentic relationships you need to succeed without losing sight of who you are. The business pressures you to present yourself in a "sales friendly" way. Trying to be someone everyone will like leaves you unsure of who you really are and afraid to express your authentic self for fear of losing a sale. I spent years navigating these pressures before I was forced to pause and take stock of what really mattered.

I never intended to go into real estate. In fact, it was my sister, Marti, who convinced me to give it a try. She "sold" me by focusing on what she knew would resonate with me—I could help people and provide them the support they needed through a transition in their lives. Real estate can be the largest investment people make, and Realtors® get to make a huge difference. Those were all things I valued. So, I went to real estate school at night while working full time as a computer programmer. I passed my tests and started my real estate career.

While Marti was right about what working in real estate *could* be, I realized very quickly it would be hard to focus on helping people with the immense pressure to always "fill the pipeline." I held open houses every weekend and hoped for a parade of people I didn't know. I knocked on doors of people I had never met and cold-called strangers. These were the playbook strategies, and my managers kept telling me to follow the plan and the systems to be successful. I continued to follow their advice and focused on the next sale, the next prospect. I felt like a hamster running on a wheel. If I was helping people, I didn't get to see it because I never got to know them. The authentic connections were missing, and I was scrambling to meet someone else's definition of success while ignoring my own, but then my world changed forever.

On May 16, 2007, I found my sister, Marti, dead on the floor of her bedroom. We had just spent the previous Sunday together with our mom for Mother's Day. Marti had taken time off to cook Mom a special meal, and after eating, I had to leave early for work. I left the two of them at the dining room table, and it never occurred to me that I might not see my sister again. Everything was different from that moment on—even if I wasn't ready to admit it yet. I tried to hold on to the lifestyle I had created with Marti's insistence. I rehabbed a house for myself and was at the peak of my real estate career when Marti passed away. I had been working alongside my dad, and we were splitting our closings fifty/fifty. Losing a child is the hardest thing for a parent to experience and Dad never really came back to work after Marti died. He mostly stayed at home to take care of Mom, who was devastated by this loss.

I continued to give my dad half of every closing, but it became clear that he wasn't going to be returning to the business. Marti had convinced me to get into this business to help others, but now she was gone. I had worked alongside my dad, creating a supportive partnership, but now that was gone, too. When the real estate market crashed at the end of 2007, I was on my own to try to stay afloat.

In addition to facing professional consequences of the market crash, I was also facing personal ones. After two years of scrambling, fighting, and stressing to modify the loan to keep my house, I was ready to let go and go with the flow. I decided to sell my house short sale. I received my first foreclosure letter within a week of letting the lender know I was done trying to modify my loan. It's terrifying to have the comfort and security of your home ripped away. People were telling me that "the bank" would bar my doors and prevent me from entering my own house. I was concerned for the safety of my animals, two dogs and a cat, who were my "children" and my primary concern. I learned that filing for bankruptcy would stop the threat of foreclosure by the bank and would only be accepted by the courts IF I were able to afford my house payment. But I had been trying to modify my loan for the very reason of not being able to afford my house payment. Still, if I wanted to sell my house, the bankruptcy would 'delay' the foreclosure from happening and buy me time to sell, which would be the best-case scenario for me.

I never imagined I would be uttering the two words "foreclosure" and "bankruptcy," and I was very humbled and worried about becoming homeless. I remember walking by a homeless person and thinking to myself, "We really are not that far away from each other." I was embarrassed. I showed up to the courthouse with a paralegal I had never met. We sat in a huge room. The court official kept the same stern face every time she struck the gavel. When my turn came, I approached her, and she covered the microphone and said, "I know you; are you Marti's sister?" When I said yes, she smiled. "I remember you! You came with Marti to our Toastmasters group." She read the notes in my file and softly said that she could not accept my request for bankruptcy because of the monthly house payment. I took a deep sigh of relief knowing this would stop the foreclosure attempt and give me time to sell my house. I felt like Marti was watching over me, and the fact that I knew the court official felt like a gentle comforting hug from Marti.

I learned to focus on what I wanted to create. Whenever a disempowering thought popped into my mind, I thanked that thought for sharing, cleared my mind and re-focused on the necessary next actions. As I thought about what I might want in a future new home, I got a call from a past client who had inherited a house and needed a renter. The house exceeded my list of wants, and I ended up living there four years, helping to oversee the house's rehab. I was burnt out. My real estate business had a few meaningful moments of success, but mostly I felt exhausted by the "work" of real estate. I had lost my connection with my clients. My personal health spiraled. I was at my heaviest weight. Between the grief of losing my sister and the stress of losing my house, I had been neglecting myself.

It was 2012, and I began to recall my passion for being an athlete. That same year, the team I played on in 1983, S & T University Women's Soccer Team, was inducted into the Athletic Hall of Fame. Memories of winning that honor myself in 2002, for being an accomplished Goalkeeper, came flooding back. I knew I needed to get active again and become the athlete I wanted to be. My love of dance and movement led me to discover Zumba, and I became a Zumba-certified instructor for a few years. I also tried kickboxing and became a certified instructor and taught kickboxing. Yet, while

I was inspiring other women to start Zumba and kickboxing, I was struggling to pay my bills.

My brother, Scott, suggested I get a job somewhere—anywhere!—to receive benefits and a steady income. I interviewed with the two places I enjoyed being: the gym and Whole Foods. I spent the next two and a half years working in the Whole Foods Market Customer Service Department. I learned about food, how to be a personal shopper, and raised over $26,000 for non-profit organizations. I met my partner there, but things weren't smooth sailing just yet. This period of time was a new normal in my life and was what I needed to remember why I had gone into business in the first place. Just like Marti had envisioned, I enjoyed making a huge difference in people's lives while living an authentic life.

On June 6, 2015, I broke my left pinky moving furniture at home—I say that's how I "broke" back into real estate full time. I was raising money for airfare for a non-profit trip to help build a schoolhouse for deaf children in Colombia. Although I continued to work through the pain, I wasn't able to fulfill my job responsibilities. I went to the doctor to take care of my pinky, and the next day a past client called me to help them sell their house.

Determination and resilience, with a sprinkling of luck, paved the way for my return to real estate. With a new thirst to reinvent myself as a Realtor and to make a difference in the lives of people, I began to create my new life. I now celebrate every June 6th as "Pinky Day" for being the catalyst to the success I didn't even know was awaiting me.

I had no car, but I learned to ask for and receive help. I'd borrow a car for a few hours on a Sunday afternoon to show houses. My phone was ringing all the time and within two months, I bought a car. By the end of the year, I had sold $2.5 million in real estate and created a new brand representing my authentic self. Everything leading up to that moment served a purpose and gave me a new perspective. I was soon back in real estate full time.

The very first sale I made was for a couple I had met fifteen years earlier. Dee had come through my Whole Foods Market line over the years. She always said they were going to call me when they were ready to move, and they did. This experience was the blueprint for my new approach: create meaningful relationships with people who loved the authentic me. I no longer tried to "fill the pipeline" with strangers. Instead, I focused on nurturing and creating authentic relationships. My business grew through word of mouth and referrals—people who appreciated my wealth of experience, knowledge, and authenticity.

Another huge gift I received was learning the importance of my own hobbies and passions—filling myself with joy, happiness and bliss—the foundation I needed to give back to others. I played softball back in the 1994 Gay Games, and my team won the gold medal. Pickleball became a huge passion of mine. Through pickleball, I reconnected with Chris, and his wife, Gina—who I played soccer with, in college. As we connected over our shared passion, I was able to help Chris and Gina purchase their first investment property.

Inspired by a conga drum I saw in my sister's home after she died, I found another new passion: making clay pottery Udu drums. I met Natalie at the studio during clay class. We became fast friends, and she asked for my business card. Her sister and brother-in-law were moving and needed help selling their house and buying a new one. My authentic connection with Natalie led to another opportunity to make a huge difference in their lives.

Where I once felt pressured to keep the real estate business separate from who I really was, I now proudly portray my "woo-woo" self wherever I go—and the business follows. I've learned many life lessons since restarting my real estate business and how I feel impacts the life I create. Now I choose wisely where to put my focus and energy. My first priority is to my health, wellness, and happiness. There are 1,440 minutes each day, and I get to choose how many I will spend happy. I am happiest when I honor my multi-faceted authentic self, vibrationally attracting the perfect people, and creating real connections.

Lisa Frumhoff is a Realtor® in St. Louis, MO and her business success is rooted in creating authentic personal relationships. By embracing the things that fill her with joy and purpose, she builds genuine trust and connection with those around her. She believes working in real estate is about helping people through times of transition and she prides herself on really getting to know her clients so that success is defined by the journey they take together.

Lisa believes unexpected doors open when your heart is fully immersed in your daily interactions and the blending of her professional and personal worlds is a testament to that reality. Lisa aims to help others live authentically and joyfully by embracing their own meaningful relationships, and she hopes that others starting out in the business world will use their own passions and interests as a foundation for their work.

In addition to her business, Lisa loves to play pickleball, spend time with her partner and pets, and create Udu drums by hand. Lisa is a certified Reiki Master and brings her belief in people's spiritual- and energy-connections into every aspect of her life.

Lisa@LisaFrumhoff.com
www.LisaFrumhoff.com
www.lisafrumhoff.com/posts

www.facebook.com/LisaFrumhoffRealEstate/
www.linkedin.com/in/lisafrumhoff
www.instagram.com/lisafrumhoff/
www.youtube.com/lisafrumhoff

I Have Met the Enemy and He Is Us.

–Pogo

"KWYK, Inc." is my corporation's name. With the first package delivered to that entity, the UPS delivery man thought that he was looking for a radio station. But to me, as an accidental entrepreneur, the name has a more significant meaning than a clever and easily remembered acronym. I came up with this as my business name after a good friend offered this valuable piece of advice: "Know What You Know."

At age fifty-six, I was employed as chief financial officer/chief operating officer (CFO/COO) by a business where I intended to remain until retirement. The business was and is an escrow closing and title insurance agency. With the real estate downturn due to the housing crisis of 2008, the company became financially troubled and went up for sale upon the demand of the bank. In my capacity as CFO/COO at the time, I assembled the packages for potential buyer review. Most of the potential buyers were not local, so an element of the potential buyers' requirements was my agreement to remain and supervise the operation after the sale. Since I did not crave a change in careers, I agreed to offer my continued employment in the sales presentation package.

In a conversation with a venture capitalist about the sale of the company, I expressed my willingness to continue in my current position because I was concerned about the future of my thirty co-workers. After the end of the conversation, the business consultant who was brokering the transaction advised me that I should "Never tell a venture capitalist that you care about the employees. Tell them that you are interested in making money." I replied, "Why haven't you asked me to buy the company?"

And, indeed, the current owner had wanted that to happen, but did not want to pressure me into a decision. He knew me well enough to know that, if it was something I wanted, I would not be afraid to suggest it. With an attorney, who was a family friend and who wanted to see me be successful, along with a lender, who was willing to keep the loan in-house, and a local payoff lender, who knew I was the most likely bidder to complete the transaction, I started the journey.

On June 19, 2012, I owned a company. I signed the closing documents secure in the fantasy that, with a reduced debt service, a little time, a good business plan, and a recovering economy, we would be on a trajectory straight back to economic health. On June 20, I received a call that we had lost a customer that accounted for ten percent of our business. Although I had received excellent legal advice on how to organize my company so that I would not be responsible for all of the financial and legal responsibilities of the old company, I had underestimated the difficulty in navigating the viewpoint of vendors and customers who did not care that I was not legally obligated. I soon found out that the staff, who had not had a raise in six years and had watched layoffs of more than fifty percent of their co-workers, were overworked and fearful. Oh, no. Now what?

In retrospect, I can say that I could not have read a different book or implemented a different philosophy that would have garnered a better result than listening to friends and subject-matter experts. Fortunately, during the process of the old company's sale negotiations, I was introduced to turnaround experts and consultants who became trusted advisors. They introduced me to other experts and advisors who began guiding me through intense and sometimes painful management training.

I did not find the answers to my personal achievement in a single book or wrapped up in a single philosophy. My progress has been a result of a gathering of suggestions and techniques from multiple sources. It has been a collection of principles and philosophies that have helped me to adhere to my own values, as well as to operate effectively.

What were those tidbits of advice and words of encouragement that brought my company and me through seven years of improvement and growth? I will share them with you.

"Don't blame your family for reacting badly to your decision to be an entrepreneur; you are the one who has upset their lives."

I struggled with the skepticism my friends and family showed at my choice to be an entrepreneur. Once I realized that they were only insecure and afraid of a huge change that I had made for our future, I was able to have meaningful conversations with them.

> ### *"Just because you say I'm stupid,*
> ### *doesn't make me stupid."*

That phrase was the first I remember of the words of a woman who could stand up to a man in the sixties. My mother said it and she meant it. I still replay those words in my head when I need to respond calmly rather than defensively to a criticism.

> ### *"When are you going to use what you've learned working*
> ### *for people who don't value you enough?"*

This phrase came from my daughter. She grew up with a mother who worked long hours with minimal financial rewards. As a people-pleaser and fixer, I was drawn to positions where my help was needed and where the principals were not in a financial position to compensate me. I held the belief and expressed to my family that I was getting experience at a higher level than I would have gotten in a cookie-cutter corporate position. In some circumstances, I allowed myself to be a doormat. The doormat characteristic which was easily recognized by one of my advisors took me straight to…

> ### *"Nobody likes a martyr, so stop acting like a martyr."*

That statement can be described as an introduction to a very painful part of my management training. As I said, I was a people-pleaser. I offered my help when it wasn't requested. I wanted everyone to agree with what I suggested. Ultimately, I was asked if that behavior was working out for me. I had to admit that I often wondered how I could give so much and get so little cooperation or appreciation. I resented how much of my own life I was giving up for others. I cried the day that I figured out that all of this help I had given others came from motives that were not so generous.

"Act like an adult."

I could write an entire book around my struggles with reactions to adult issues based on childlike beliefs. My adult mind-set had been shaped by learning that emotions are illogical and nonsensical. The journey back to the origins of emotional and childlike reactions put things in a new perspective. I will forever view the therapy process in a different light. My previous beliefs only allowed me to look at it as a way to fix a broken part of you. Now I see it as a path to leading a more fulfilled adult life.

"You can continue doing things this way, but it's going to kill you."

This one stopped me in my tracks. The statement was figuratively, as well as literally, true. Right then and there, I decided to be coachable. I'm not always easily coachable, but I no longer immediately reject ideas. Stubbornness and narrow viewpoints do not seem like values for which I should give my life.

"Work on your company, not in your company."

After hearing this so often in personal coaching sessions and classes I have taken, I believe that this struggle is one that many entrepreneurs face. We have done good jobs and we are drawn to continue doing the tasks at which we are good. Shaping good managers took time and was often painful for even the best and most dedicated employees who found themselves faced with brand new situations of managing those who were formerly co-workers. It was excruciating for me too, but possible once I learned to…

Trust, but verify.

I think I'm logical, so I think my ideas are obvious to others. I now know that is just plain wrong. Once I learned (I learned it but still don't always do it) to make instructions clear, set deadlines, and follow with a check-in on progress, I was more comfortable with letting it go. The more communication I have had with employees, I have realized that…

Employees want to do a good job.

I can't speak for all employees everywhere, but I do not know a single one in my company now that doesn't want to do a good job. Employees, however, do not have a big picture viewpoint and, without appropriate feedback, have no idea of the quality or quantity of their activities and that their own activities contribute to overall success. I still am poor at feedback. So, I have hired an outside human resources consultant to challenge me to improve my communications skills with employees.

Don't let anyone throw a dead cat into your office.

This one is easy to remember, and it almost immediately impacted my daily management life. Solving a problem alone is not effective for me; I know that I see the problem only from my own viewpoint. If someone brings a problem (dead cat) and tosses it into my office, I ask for input as to how the problem might be solved. Both sides come out knowing the likelihood of a quick solution.

There are ideas and then there are GOOD ideas.

As soon as I owned a business, the solicitations from outside and suggestions from the inside came flowing in. From one viewpoint or another, many of them made sense. Since limited resources were a fact in my life, I had to narrow the implementation of new ideas to those with a high chance of quick success balanced with those that would have a yield over time. The really good ideas were beneficial to the overall health of the company.

Emotion always runs up the budget.

My business ownership is personal to me. It's hard to keep from investing in things I like instead of things that the business needs. Sometimes, my reward to myself for hard work is that the business does get a more expensive brand of lipstick. But I can't lose sight of the limited resources.

If you have an intention, set yourself up for success.

This recommendation is one that I use almost daily. The articles I read, the experts I consult, the classes that I still attend, give me the tools to achieve my goals. It works in personal life, too. If I really want to get together with an old friend, I don't just express the desire anymore; I actually ask them to help me set the date.

Be careful about which things you become involved in.

This advice came from an entrepreneurial colleague based on his own experience. Having opportunities to be on boards and involved personally in charitable efforts was risky business for me. Fortunately, I was so busy at first that I wasn't able to overcommit. Now that my business has matured and needs me less, I can enjoy more of the outside involvement.

*****

All of the lessons I have just shared have come from trusted advisors and friends. They have supported me in my life as an entrepreneur and have reminded me that I can imagine something big and live right into it as long as I don't get in my own way. My employees have gotten a raise each year and have grown from thirty to forty-five in number since I purchased the company. We have expanded from four to nine (looking at number ten) locations. And now, as I begin my succession planning, I look forward to a new phase.

As I age, the lessons that I have learned will help me to create a new work life that I cherish and appreciate. I am more peaceful than I can ever remember being in my lifetime. I wonder if this would have been the result had I not accidentally become an entrepreneur.

Jackie Hoyt is President and CEO of KWYK, Inc. dba Hillsboro Title Company. Hillsboro Title Company has eight offices and serves all types of partners involved in real estate transactions.

Jackie attended UMSL and received a BSBA with an area of concentration in Accounting. After graduation she worked for a pre-recorded music wholesaler and later owned a small pre-recorded music retail store. Her next few years were spent working for a CPA as a staff accountant. She began working part time in the bookkeeping department of Hillsboro Title Co. in May 1998. In 2012, at the age of 56, Jackie purchased the assets of Hillsboro Title Co., Inc. and began operating it with the intent of creating a business that was noteworthy in an industry where the product of title insurance does not, in itself, have many distinguishing characteristics.

Although Hillsboro Title has grown, Jackie believes that the company's identity should reflect a personal brand of service along with a professionalism that instills confidence in its customers in both small and large transactions. Marketing efforts are centered on community and service.

jackieh@hillsborotitle.com
www.hillsborotitle.com

www.facebook.com/HillsboroTitle/
www.linkedin.com/company/hillsboro-title-company
www.twitter.com/hillsborotitle

Networking That Works

Can networking ever be fun? You bet it can—if you want it to be. Networking is a necessity. Research indicates networking leads to more jobs, business opportunities, and higher productivity. Building and nurturing authentic relationships, both professionally and personally, can also improve work and job satisfaction!

Flashback a couple of years ago and I would NEVER have envisioned I would be networking. Me, the girl who is more comfortable at home than in a crowd and buries her nose in a book rather than get all dressed up to go out and meet people. Me, who most of my life struggled to make friends and have any kind of conversation. When I moved to St. Louis a little over three years ago, I dreaded it. I started working at the Hispanic Chamber of Commerce and realized I was going to have to be comfortable meeting lots of new people.

I can't say that I figured it all out, but I can share a few things that have worked for me. These strategies have helped me become more comfortable meeting new people and making friends.

What Is Networking?

I think I was in college the first time I heard about networking; and thinking back, the word still conjures up all kinds of emotions. Let's start with the facts: Networking is about meeting new people and building relationships which lead to other relationships, which lead to possibilities.

Why Is Networking So Hard?

Networking puts us outside of our comfort zone. I get it. I'm always afraid I won't connect with anyone, or if I do, what will we talk about? It also doesn't help when I stare at my phone while networking, hoping for an email or text message to come through. Be sure to put the phone away! More than anything, I think networking is hard because of all of the pressure we put on ourselves. We focus too much on the business cards and how we introduce ourselves; we think too much about who can help us when all that is required is to smile and be you! It's time to start building real relationships and change our perspective from "Is this a potential client?" or "Can they get me a job?" to "How much value can we provide one another?" Since realizing this, I started focusing more on the value I could offer—whether it was an introduction, a book recommendation, or marketing advice for a small business owner—and suddenly, it was easier and more fun to meet new people.

Let's do this! It's time to step outside our comfort zone. Meeting people can be fun, so allow me to offer a couple of strategies to help both online and in person.

Networking At Events

I used to think I had to keep the conversation going by asking questions or that I had to know the latest sports results or headline news. For many years, I tried that, and it wasn't fun. Think about it. What is it that helps us form a connection and start a friendship?

Simple: Introducing myself and getting to know the person I was speaking to. Once we started talking about a topic they were passionate about, the next step was listening. Remember to *listen to understand, not to reply.* Listening allows us to connect and build relationships.

When I started at the Hispanic Chamber of Commerce, it was ROUGH. I had to go to a lot of work and industry events which I dreaded. When we hosted events, people would often find me behind the registration table, delaying being thrown into the crowd. Eventually, I slowly would greet one person after another; and before I knew it, the event was over, and I had survived!

When attending other events, I'd look for a friendly face (either one I knew or one who had the same look of fear on their face) and introduce myself. "Hi. How are you? I'm Gabriela," I'd say, and I'd leave it open for them to introduce themselves. It was a slow process. Sometimes, the conversation died shortly after the initial introductions and we'd both move on to talk to someone else. Other times, we'd connect about the simplest things—and even though it was not always related to work, it was a way of building trust. It got easier as I started to gain confidence in myself and the key was to look for opportunities to help others.

Perhaps the following tips might help at your next event:
- Introduce people to others that you know in the room who could be a good connection
- Invite them to an upcoming event or workshop
- Recommend a good book or movie

More Tips for Wary Introverts

If you hear the word "networking" and it makes you want to run in the other direction, I get it! Being social truly does wear us introverts out. Here are tips that helped me on many occasions and perhaps they will help you to get the most out of these events:

- Arrive early when the crowd is smaller. It will be easier for you to start conversations. The first time I realized this worked, I arrived early by accident to a construction breakfast event and enjoyed how easy it was to connect to others just based on the fact that we were all early to the party.

- Be realistic and set an attainable goal of making meaningful connections. When it's all over, remember to reward yourself and head home to finish your favorite book or movie. After recently attending an all-day symposium, I found myself overwhelmed by the full day of conversations and exchanges. To take care of myself when I got home, I made sure to watch one of my latest Hulu episodes before I got back to the business cards I had exchanged. The reward helped me clear my head and allowed me to approach my follow-up plan with a positive attitude and a clear head.

Be Vulnerable and Ask for Help

When I moved to St. Louis in 2016, I did not know anyone. I had just started my job and realized that, in order to help my clients, I would need to know who to connect them to. Who were the resources available to help them scale their business or get access to capital? On a whim, I reached out to my network in Detroit, sharing with them my recent move and my new position. I asked them if they knew anyone in St. Louis that they would recommend I meet. Lo and behold, the introductions started immediately; and I have been connected to many of those people and organizations ever since. Those initial contacts have been some of my biggest cheerleaders and advocates. They helped me connect to others in the extended business ecosystem. Be sure to reach out to those you know, regardless of where they are, and ask for help.

Volunteer to Be a Host

Before you say no to hosting, hear me out. Being a host allows you to take on a different role. It may be a little outside your comfort zone, but just think of all of the pre-event contacts you will make. As one of the event's planners, you'll be walking into the event with pre-made connections.

I had the chance to host my niece's baby shower recently, and I really enjoyed the change in having guests introduce themselves to me rather than the other way around. In a room full of mostly strangers, this gave me the freedom to not feel the stress of creating small talk and introducing myself to complete strangers because we had already exchanged emails and other pleasantries during the time leading up to the event.

Online Networking to the Rescue

Online Networking has been a game changer and an opportunity for me to connect, to build relationships without stress and in the comfort of my own home—thanks to social media. Pick your favorite platform and find your voice. LinkedIn lets me "like" and comment on others' posts and pictures. I feel engaged without the usual pressure. I have also been able to share my thoughts on some of my favorite subjects which have started online conversations allowing me to connect with other like-minded people. Networking online has also been a great way to share interesting articles, inspiring pictures, and events with the people I'm connected to directly. I can easily forward information to them, and they appreciate the resource.

Social media can also be a great source for conversations. Using hashtags and checking out industry influencers on social media can arm you with the latest information that might help you get off on the right foot at your next event. Using social media also offers an amazing opportunity for following up with people you've met, as well as new opportunities to find and engage with people who aren't local.

Practice Does Make Perfect

"Networking is a lot like nutrition and fitness: we know what to do, the hard part is making it a top priority."

–Herminia Ibarra

Practice. Before you know it, you won't even think "I'm networking"; you'll be meeting and connecting with people without overthinking it. You'll have found a way of doing it that works for you. But first you must practice. It's time to get out and try some of the tips I have shared.

Try Small Events and Larger Events

Small or large breakfast and evening events can exercise your networking muscles. Meeting new people at the dog park has been a great way to practice my networking without the pressure of work—and we get to talk about one of our favorite subjects, our fur babies. I have also recently found breakfasts to be really enjoyable and without the expectation of drinks and heavy appetizers (which my trainer appreciates!). I have started to find a new appreciation for early morning networking.

Follow-Up

Part of networking also includes following up. If you are interested in exploring more with a contact, ask them for coffee or perhaps offer your expertise or make a referral and introduction. It's easy for me to get busy and sometimes just not feel like attending an event. Make a habit of attending regularly—an excellent strategy for overcoming anxiety. Make a conscious effort to attend every meeting you have RSVP'd to, and you'll be astounded at how quickly you start to feel comfortable. Don't forget that establishing connections is just the first part of the process. You want to make sure you stay engaged with any new contacts, both offline and online. I have actually been able to become friends with some of the connections and form long-lasting relationships that aren't just work-related. Having a system in place to follow up is important to ensure you keep the conversation going.

Adding business cards to your contact list and not just letting them stack up on your desk is the first step. I like the Evernote app's ability to scan each card and add them to my phone contacts. Make it a priority to add all of your new connections to your main contact list and then engage further. Some suggestions might include:

- Connect on Social Media—This has been an easy way for me to keep the conversation going.
- Send an email, a handwritten note, or an interesting article related to something you may have discussed.

- Offer to get coffee together or grab lunch. Even if they're not available, they'll remember that you made the effort.

As you start to more easily navigate business after hours, golf outings, fundraisers, and the like, you will see your comfort soar. The more often you practice your networking skills, the more often you will find the possibilities become limitless. As you continue to grow and learn, you will find yourself looking forward to events and opportunities to connect.

Alas, there are no shortcuts. Simply trust the process and operate in excellence. Building real relationships takes time, patience, skill, and the willingness to put yourself into new situations. So, get out there and flex your networking muscles!

 A native of Guanajuato, México, Gabriela Ramírez-Arellano helps entrepreneurs and small business owners launch and gain access to capital and opportunities for growth. She spends her days helping small business owners reach their goals.

Recognized as a thought-leader in social innovation and entrepreneurship, Gabriela was named a Diverse Business Leader and one of the Top 100 people to know in St. Louis. Her goal to conquer her fear of public speaking and networking motivated her to be featured on St. Louis Public Radio, the STL101 Speaking Series, on various food entrepreneurship panels, as well as several keynotes addressing women's leadership.

She is on the board of the BALSA Foundation, Contractor Loan Fund, Fontbonne Arts and Science Advisory, St. Louis Equity and Inclusion Collective, St. Louis Council of Construction Consumers Diversity Committee, United Way Multicultural Leadership Society, and several others. She and her husband own Don Emiliano's Restaurante Mexicano in O'Fallon, MO and she co-hosts the Auténtico Podcast to empower and showcase bilingual Latinx professionals and small business owners. Gabriela holds a BS in Marketing from the University of Missouri, Columbia, and an MBA from Lindenwood University.

gramirezarellano@hccstl.com
www.hccstl.com
www.balsafoundation.org
www.donemilianos.com

Continued on next page

www.facebook.com/GabrielaRamirezArellano
www.linkedin.com/in/gabrielaramirezarellano
www.twitter.com/gabyrdarris
www.instagram.com/gabyrdarris

Live, Work, and Play with a Twist of Inspiration

Everything I have lived through and accomplished has been achieved because of hard work, tenacity, dedication, determination, drive, and passion. Nothing came easy for me, and I've had to deal with one challenge after another. I've always said, "If I wasn't actually living this life, I honestly wouldn't believe it." It amazes me how one person can endure so much pain and heartbreak, yet still be filled with an abundant amount of hope, faith, love and joy.

I describe my life as a bittersweet, action-packed, adventurous Disney movie with many ups, downs, twists, turns, U-turns, roundabouts, and detours along the way—and just like with all great Disney movies, in the end, things seem to work out perfectly, as I always get my "Happily Ever After." I have now learned to just trust the process and enjoy the ride along the way.

As a stubborn, Italian/Greek Jersey Girl, and proud Leo the Lioness, what you see is what you get. I am genuine, authentic, hardworking, and determined to succeed. Business is not just business to me, it is personal. I conduct business the way I live my life—with honesty, loyalty, passion, and heart. I am a person of my word; I always walk my talk and own my shortcomings and mistakes; I never point fingers or make excuses; I learn the lessons at hand and try to constantly improve.

I was working in a nursing home thirty-two hours a week and bartending in a night club on the weekends. I was twenty-two years old and pregnant. My doctor put me on disability, as I was considered high risk, and I was no longer able to perform my nursing or bartending duties. There I was—sitting at home—and for a girl who had worked since age twelve, doing nothing was not an option.

My father owned a construction company, and he offered me a position working eight to five behind a desk. I had never considered a desk job; however, this seemed like a better option than sitting home doing absolutely nothing for the next seven months. I was hired as a service coordinator, and I was trying to pretend I knew what I was doing. Unfortunately, I had zero knowledge of construction; and within the first few weeks, I had embarrassed myself terribly and totally fell on my face.

I had many lessons to learn, including…

Lesson No. 1:
If You Do Not Know Something, Ask.

From that moment on, I became a "Curious George," as I never wanted to look stupid again. I started asking lots of questions to learn as much as I could. I worked in that department for two years, eventually transitioning to the construction side of the company in the estimating department as an estimating coordinator, also taking over the business development/marketing responsibilities as well. I became the face of the company. It was a challenging time for me: not only was I learning a new position in a new industry, but I was a woman in construction. I was determined to succeed so

I listened, asked lots of questions, and constantly challenged myself to learn and grow.

Lesson No. 2:
Be Authentic, Be True to
Your Core Essence. Be You.

My next lesson in the business world was at my first Retail Contractors Association meeting. I looked around the room and thought to myself, "How am I going to sell our company when there are one hundred other people in this room who are doing the same exact thing as me? The answer I was given from God was "You"—the answer was me—I was what was different.

We are all unique. Being "you" is the key differentiator and that helps us stand apart. People do business with people based on trust and relationships. Always represent yourself first and foremost, then, secondly, the company you represent. Your name, your word, your reputation is on the line, you get one so do what feels right.

Utilizing the people-skills I had learned as a former bartender and nurse, I began to walk around the room introducing myself as "Jersey Gina." Life had taught me the patience to listen and learn; and paired with my love for helping people, I began building new business relationships. My intuitive empathy, strong emotional intelligence skills, and my ability to be kind, friendly, and curious served me well.

Having helped to grow our company and many years of being the director of the estimating dept, I found myself battling Lyme Disease and after fifteen years of wearing many hats in a family-owned and operated business, I decided it was time to make a life-altering decision and leave the family business. I needed a break, and I wanted to have a father/daughter rather than employer/employee relationship. My favorite quote and my hardest life lesson, "If you always do what you've always done, you will always get what you've always got" (the true definition of insanity).

Bringing fifteen years' worth of relationships and my trusted reputation, I accepted a position as executive director of business development with an architectural firm—another family-owned and operated business, just not my family—where I could learn the front end/design aspect of the industry. My goal was to eventually go back and buy out my father to create a design-build firm.

Within the first year and a half, I brought in thirty-three national retail clients. I gave my heart and soul growing this company. Unfortunately, after four and a half years of hard work growing their business, I was terminated. I was heartbroken, embarrassed, and totally devastated. What made it even worse was their attempt to tarnish my reputation that I had worked very hard to build and maintain for over twenty years.

Lesson No. 3:
Take Off Those Rose-Colored Glasses.

It was April 2015 and my entire outlook on business, people, and life changed. I was not only managing my professional career struggle, I was also now managing a severe illness, Lupus, made worse by stress and drama. Having been hospitalized seven times in one month, I was beat up, let down, and losing hope.

While everyone loves you in good times, it's the rough times when you need the loyalty of others. Not many will be there, and some will even turn their backs because they worry about what others think. I was unemployed, feeling alone, unsure of how to handle life, and defending myself against a business owner and some of his employees. I had one girlfriend who never left my side during this time. She felt terrible, and in some way partially responsible for my termination. But for the most part it was just me. I learned those who are with you are for you and those who are not with you are not, I had to see many peoples' true colors; and although it honestly hurt me to see the truth, I grew wiser and stronger with each challenge. I learned to be courageous enough to stand alone and be okay.

Lesson No. 4:
Be Courageous Enough to Stand Alone.

I honored my one-year contract of non-compete and took time off to go through the grieving process of being terminated. Having a bruised ego, I was mad, sad, angry, hurt—it really was an emotional roller coaster. I continued to be me: out networking in the industry, attending the conferences, and volunteering for the various boards and committees. During this time, all my former clients were coming to me to access various vendors, and those same vendors were asking me for introductions to former clients. I kept hearing the word "connect" in my head and feeling as if I needed to create a business, but I didn't want to monetize my heart OR FAIL.

Lesson No. 5:
Just Do It. Go. Take Action.

Having been fired and living with all the drama that had been directed my way, I lost self-confidence. I doubted myself, so starting a business was scary. I did not want to fail, yet I somehow found the courage to stand alone and just do it!

Lesson No. 6:
Make Your Own Lemonade.

As we've all heard, when you are served lemons, make lemonade. Not just any ole' lemonade—make it your own creation, unique and special with your very own twist of you. That's exactly what I did!

I created my own consulting firm: Connect Source Consulting Group, LLC (CSCG). It was a gift from God and has a special meaning behind the company name for me, I am connected to Source Energy, a/k/a, God. I allow that divine, loving, positive energy to flow through me so that I may consult with and help others. I specialize in the design and construction industry, bridging the gaps by connecting the dots and the right people for successful projects. I have a "work and play with a twist of inspiration" business model. The "twist" being the foundation of conscious capitalism—doing business with a higher purpose to elevate all of humanity. Every contract I receive, I donate a portion to a non-profit near and dear to my heart as a reflection of my true passion for helping others. My hope is to inspire others to focus on their passion and higher purpose so as to engage and energize all stakeholders. By bringing stakeholders and businesses together in a common cause, we create value and win together.

I believe my current success within my industry is due to being one hundred percent integrated from the start. Starting at the bottom and wearing so many hats provided me firsthand knowledge and understanding of everyone's roles within the entire construction process. I love working with people and building collaborative, winning teams, working together with shared core values and mission for the best interest of our clients. We either all win or we all lose since we are all in this together, so play nice in the playground. By helping each other throughout the process, we are all stronger and more likely to succeed together. I believe this collaboration over competition business strategy has worked to my advantage and is a huge part of my success. I attribute my relationships and network to allowing me to get to where I am today. There is no better compliment than when your competition recommends you or comes to you for assistance!

Lesson No.7:
Create Your Own Lane.

My "work and play with a twist of inspiration" business model put me over the top and helped me rise above, to soar with success! Someone once told me to stay in my lane, which, at the time, rubbed me the wrong way. As a female in a male-dominated industry, I reflected on his comment and thought, "Not only will I not stay in my lane, but I am going to create my very own lane!" That is exactly what I did!

As I now look back on my life, the termination was the best thing that ever happened to me. It allowed me to create and bring my dreams to reality now as I look forward to my third year of entrepreneurship.

I like to say, "From breakdown lane to an open-road lane—without any end—with lots of freedom and many opportunities!" There are no traffic jams along the extra mile. I not only go the extra mile, but I do everything with passion and from my heart. I truly believe this is what sets me apart from the rest.

Lesson No. 8:
Helping and Serving Others—
Doing Business with Heart.

I work straight from my heart. My success now comes by helping people and businesses grow, and that makes my heart sing. My mission is showing others how to lead from their heart, which leads to a better way of doing business and a better way to live life, overall.

I work hard and play hard, and that makes me happy. Everyone wants to work with happy people. Happier people work harder, have more fun while doing it, and are much more successful. Add in a twist of inspiration by doing business to help others and you find fulfillment through your higher purpose.

I encourage you to listen to your heart, have fun, and believe in yourself and your dreams. I am living proof that you can create the life of your dreams. If you believe it, you will see it!

Gina Marie is the Founder & Principal Consultant of Connect Source Consulting Group, LLC., she specializes in outsourced Business Development & Management Consulting, helping individuals and businesses get to the next level. Her company is based on the foundation of Conscious Capitalism, doing business with HEART to elevate all of humanity, every contract that she receives she donates to something that is near and dear to her heart.

Her mission is to show others not only a better way to do business, how to lead from within and do business from your HEART, with purpose of helping others. She loves to empower and inspire others to have fun, to live their passion, to create and live the life that they dream of. People, Purpose, Passion, Planet, Profit, WIN-WIN-WIN for everyone!!!

Some fun personal facts about her: She enjoys living life to the fullest, dancing, singing, listening to music, being on a beach in the sun, loves live entertainment—music, concerts, sporting events, yoga, spiritual practices, spending time with her two children, traveling, trying new things and volunteering to help others in any way she can.

gina@connectscg.com
www.connectscg.com

www.facebook.com/ggnoda
www.linkedin.com/in/gina-marie-noda
www.twitter.com/NJGirlG

Think Bigger. Be Different. Bring Value.

Think Bigger: Be Ambitious in the Scale of Change You Think Is Possible.

Back in the dark ages, three years before the iPhone launched when the BlackBerry was the cutting edge of corporate mobile technology, I took my first job. It was a marketing position for a pharmaceutical company. Our challenge was to promote a declining prescription drug to doctors and ensure the brand stayed top of mind. The conventional methods of communication and promotion at the time included direct mail, email, sales reps, and sampling. But I had a different idea.

I had been following trends in the consumer packaged goods (CPG) industry. Marketing through mobile phones via short message services (SMS) and mobile coupons was in its nascent stage. I thought, "Why not use SMS to market to our doctors?"

There were many reasons why not, and I heard them all.

- "That's not how we do things."
- "We work in a highly regulated industry. We have to be careful about what we do."
- "That's business-to-consumer. We're business-to-business."

- "Doctors use gatekeepers. They would never give their cell phone number to a pharmaceutical sales rep!"
- "That's an invasion of privacy. It could backfire on us."

We took it up a level. Not only did we use mobile, but we launched a mobile-only loyalty program. How did I get my team on board for such a crazy idea? I asked, "What do you always pick up as you walk out the door in the morning?" The answer: "My keys and my phone."

I had a good team—in fact—the best! At that moment, they saw what I did: the massive growth in mobile devices, a compound annual growth rate of twenty-eight percent, a medium as personal as your house key, and the inevitable one hundred percent market penetration of the second screen overtaking television. We saw what the traditional business-to-business marketers hadn't yet realized: that the emerging world of mobile provided an opportunity for immediate, intimate conversations with doctors; that traditional marketing mechanisms lacked the capability to create such powerful connections.

Suddenly, we were all on the same page. Thinking bigger. It was still a gamble, though, because mobile was an emerging category and we were betting that others had underestimated its potential. The bet paid off. Doctors all over the country signed up. The loyalty program ran for two years, reviving a declining brand, doubling revenues, and winning awards at various forums for innovative use of emerging media. Real innovation generates impactful results by transcending traditional thinking and novelty. It generates results which break the barriers of expectations and obliterate the norms to create new norms.

My parents once told me, "Focus on your education. It's your one true life-long asset that stays with you." When I landed my first job, my father pulled me aside and changed the mission: "Doing a job is just following orders. Anyone can do that, but not everyone leaves something behind when they're gone. Don't just take a job. Build a legacy."

As a child, I was challenged at every turn. Maybe that's what comes from growing up in a military family, moving every two or three years, focusing on the mission. In the military, devotion to the mission transcends rank or gender, and I brought that singular focus to my team.

Success comes from the team, each contributing their strengths to achieve the goal. My contribution was to bring a vision, to focus our gaze beyond what others had done, to help create something new that could only be accomplished by a team unified in purpose and passion.

Our next challenge was to take a leading prescription medication to the over-the-counter (OTC) market. Conventional wisdom said that the transition to OTC required abandoning the prescription market, since the revenues from the larger OTC market would dwarf prescription sales.

We did all the things required to engage the OTC market— packaging changes, alternative flavors—but I advocated against foregoing the prescription sales. In my view, it's not an either/or world, it's a both/and world. After considerable discussion, we decided to sell in both markets. A decade later, the product is still a leading medication in both prescription and OTC sales. We won the chairman's award for driving innovation that delivered a significant business impact. Think Bigger than just delivering on a task, meeting deadlines, and hitting your numbers.

Some years later, my husband took a job in another city, so I resigned and we moved. I know what you're thinking, What about your career? What about your legacy? But there's something you don't know: In graduate school, my husband and I started out as a team, teasing each other about who was the smartest and challenging each other to greater accomplishments. When I landed my dream job at the top pharmaceutical company in the country, he moved right along with me. Now, years later, he had a great opportunity, and I moved right along with him. Think bigger than just yourself and your aspirations. In every aspect of your life, it takes a team.

Be Different: You Can't Create a Legacy By Blending In.

In a new city, I found a marketing position with a retail bill payment startup and stepped up to the mission of building another legacy. Things went well, but in a start-up, cash is king. Early on, we hit a rough patch, and I was asked to let go half of my team. That wasn't my idea of a legacy. I went to the CEO and said, "What if I earned my team's salary in terms of promotional budget, would I be allowed to keep my team?"

He frowned. "How would you do that?"

I smiled. "You know our budget for sales promotions?"

He nodded.

"If I can find a way to fund our promotions without touching our cash, will you let me keep my team?"

Curious, he threw down the gauntlet. "You have one quarter to get the brands lined up and show promotional funds coming in."

We were in the middle of layoffs with everyone in survival mode, emailing resumes, looking for a landing spot. My idea required buy-in from multiple internal teams, the union, and outside companies, including retailers and CPG suppliers. All on a brutally short schedule.

Several CPG companies were looking to expand their footprint to other retailers and provide samples to prospective customers. We had the connections they wanted, so my new team created a joint promotion: anyone who used our payment service at selected locations would get a freebie CPG product placed in their retail space. Imagine the scope. We powered through that quarter, every individual focused on the goal, unified by the mission. Despite challenges, we hit our goal, the promotion was extended for a year, and everyone kept their job. A leader gets nowhere without a team. In fact, without a team, there is no such thing as a leader. A team working together to execute the vision builds the legacy.

In a collaborative, nurturing setting, there is competitive value, which fosters engagement, productivity, innovation, and quality— not just for you, but for the business as well. Women are uniquely, but not exclusively, positioned to cultivate these differentiators.

I tell my team to forget about competing with their colleagues. You must be your own benchmark. Olympic athletes don't compete against each other; they compete against their previous performance. Even after receiving the gold medal, they return to work trying to beat the record they just broke.

Discover what you want to achieve, the change you want to make, the value you want to deliver. The only real metrics are the goals you set for yourself. You must aim for goals that others dare not set.

My father-in-law once told me that a tree that bears fruit always bows down. The tree that bears no fruit might wave its branches high to signal its importance, but the tree that produces visible results has no need of such posturing. It doesn't exist for its own sake. It bends down to provide shade and shelter for others. His words constantly remind me that I am not here just to serve my own interests.

Once after a big win for my team, one of my peers claimed credit for their work. My team was upset. I realized that, by letting someone else take credit, I wasn't just being humble, I was disappointing my team and my boss. My team was looking to me to be their advocate, and I had failed them. And the executives were looking to me to blaze the trail, to validate their decision to champion me. I had responsibility that went both directions. I have learned that sometimes in my success I have to step beyond my own perspective and stand up for all the stakeholders.

Bring Value: Anyone Can Fill a Slot, But Those Who Bring Value Will Be Valued.

When I came back from maternity leave, I had split priorities. I had a job to do, one that I did well, and I also had a son. On one hand, I wouldn't be able to hold to the same long hours as before my son was born, coming in early and staying late. On the other hand, if I wanted to pursue my career, I still had to drive innovation, push the boundaries, and create a legacy.

The challenge before me was to make every hour count for multiple hours. My work had to show that I was worth it, that I delivered value commensurate to my expectations.

My mother has an unfaltering confidence in my ability to push beyond what I think is possible. My childhood school divided the students into four houses and staged competitions among us. One of my classmates told my mother that I was so competitive that the other teams concentrated their best candidates away from areas in which I competed to give them a better chance of winning. Any time I face a setback or an obstacle, my mother reminds me that when I do my best, I will always find a way through.

I realized that, if I wasn't as present in the office as before my son was born, my work had to be omnipresent. If I couldn't physically be there as many hours as before, I had to make sure that the impact I made to the business was always there, making such a difference that my organization would be happy to accommodate a modified schedule because they knew it wouldn't affect my work. I remembered something important. It takes a team. My whole family stepped up—even my brother, busy with his medical studies, traveled hours when I needed help taking care of my son.

The world, consumers, and competitors are constantly changing. If you are not changing, you are losing ground. It's not about getting the next promotion; it's about developing new competencies, creating new success stories, making a tangible business impact. If you deliver value and stay relevant, advancement will come.

When I started at my current organization, HCL, as a working mother, I was hired as a team of one to market for a single industry segment. I demonstrated my value, taking nothing for granted. Four years later, I had recruited and hired fifty people and was leading marketing for six industries.

At that time, I was given the opportunity to contribute to HCL's Red Ladder initiative, winner of the 2017 Stevie awards for Women in Business. I accepted the position to help women in technology and to pay it forward. This program now spans fifty-plus customer organizations across three continents. In my nine years at HCL, the company has grown from $5 billion in revenue to a revenue run rate of $10 billion in Q3 2020. I have grown with it, receiving five promotions in that time. People seek to join my team for the vision I create, to do something new, to go the extra mile and more.

To think bigger. To be different. To bring value.

What legacy will you leave for those who follow?

 Shimona Chadha is a marketing and business strategy professional with over two decades of experience with both Fortune 1000 and start-up companies in building strong teams to drive insights-based strategy, planning, and execution.

As an award-winning marketer and general manager, Shimona has seen outstanding success in creating new markets and categories, while positioning companies for top-line, brand and market-share growth in highly competitive industries. At HCL, a $9.3 billion technology company, she heads marketing for the Retail, Consumer Packaged Goods, Telecom, Media, Entertainment, Life Sciences, Healthcare, and Professional Services verticals.

A Gold Medalist Microbiologist, Shimona also holds an MBA in marketing and finance from Symbiosis University and has attended executive leadership programs at the Yale School of Management and the Tuck School of Business.

In 2016, Shimona was chosen to lead HCL's award-winning Red Ladder initiative, a program enhancing the representation of women in leadership roles. She received The Stevie Awards for Women in Business 2017 and served on the judging committee for 2018 and 2019. She also serves on the board for the Women Future Conference and is a Leadership co-chair of both the Women's Empowerment Chapter and the Sales and Marketing Chapter of the IAOP.

shimona.chadha@gmail.com.

www.facebook.com/shimona.chadha.9
www.linkedin.com/in/shimona-chadha
www.twitter.com/shimona_chadha

WANT MORE?

ENGAGE and IGNITE
Your Business

Join BDC
group coaching

Join a BDC
roundtable

Start a BDC
roundtable in
your area

Book Erin
to speak

REACH OUT
www.blackdresscircle.com